"*Jesus Conversations* flow natura[l]
heart. He sees the insufficiencies ⌐.
brilliant truth and compassion of Jesus Christ. I'm inspired anew to share
the reasons for the hope within me, because of love."

—Kelly Monroe Kullberg, Founder, The Veritas Forum
Author of *Finding God beyond Harvard: The Quest for Veritas*

"Looking for a practical, natural way to share your faith? If so, I am confident you will both enjoy and benefit from this book. Dave Sterrett offers simple strategies all of us can use to meaningfully engage people around us in conversations about Jesus."

—Dr. Sean McDowell
Author of *Chasing Love* and *Evidence That Demands a Verdict*

"An important resource to help Christians give an answer to people who don't believe in the Bible—with the 'gentleness and respect' Jesus modeled so well."

—J. Warner Wallace, *Dateline*-featured Cold-Case Detective
Author of *Cold-Case Christianity*

"There is an enormous gap between how the Bible calls Christians to love lost people and how we actually do. If you have not shared the gospel this week, then you owe it to yourself to read *Jesus Conversations* to be inspired and trained. Dave Sterrett is not just an evangelism coach saying 'do as I say,' he lives every word and makes sharing the faith as natural as breathing."

—Jonathan "JP" Pokluda, Pastor, Harris Creek Church, Waco, Texas
Author of *Welcome to Adulting*

"There is a great need to make the gospel known to others: all others. Dave's book *Jesus Conversations* will enlighten, inspire, and instruct us to better know how to begin our gospel conversation and effectively share the hope of Jesus."

—Dr. Johnny Hunt, Vice President of Evangelism
North American Mission Board
Pastor, First Baptist Church, Woodstock, Georgia

"A hopeless world desperately needs hope. Hope has a name: Jesus. How do we have intentional conversations about him? The most important conversation we can have is a Jesus Conversation. That is why Dave's *Jesus Conversations* is such a timely book that will be relevant until Jesus comes back for his church. Get it. Read it. Share it. Discuss it."

—Shane Pruitt, national director, Next Gen Evangelism
North American Mission Board
Author of *9 Common Lies Christians Believe*

"*Jesus Conversations* is Dave's pure love for all of us to be authentic, joyful, caring, adventurous, and relevant Christians in the ever-changing culture we live in. This is not a guilt-driven book; instead, it's uniquely practical and inspiring. I'm grateful for Dave's commitment in reminding us to get outside the church walls."

—Daniel Rangel, CEO, Houston International Equipment

Jesus
Conversations

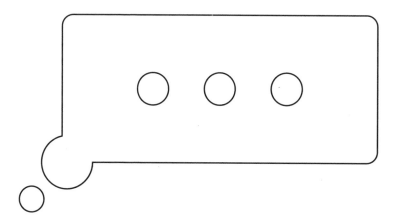

Jesus Conversations

Effective Everyday
Engagement

Dave Sterrett

HENDRICKSON
PUBLISHERS

an imprint of Hendrickson Publishing Group

Jesus Conversations: Effective Everyday Engagement

© 2021 Dave Sterrett

Published by Hendrickson Publishers
an imprint of Hendrickson Publishing Group
Hendrickson Publishers, LLC
P. O. Box 3473
Peabody, Massachusetts 01961-3473
www.hendricksonpublishinggroup.com

ISBN 978-1-68307-312-3

All rights reserved. No part of this book may be reproduced or transmitted in any form or by any means, electronic or mechanical, including photocopying, recording, or by any information storage and retrieval system, without permission in writing from the publisher.

Unless otherwise noted, Scripture quotations are taken from the Holy Bible, New International Version®, NIV®. Copyright © 1973, 1978, 1984, 2011 by Biblica, Inc.™ Used by permission of Zondervan. All rights reserved worldwide. www.zondervan.com. The "NIV" and "New International Version" are trademarks registered in the United States Patent and Trademark Office by Biblica, Inc.™

Scripture quotations marked (NLT) are taken from the Holy Bible, New Living Translation, copyright © 1996, 2004, 2015 by Tyndale House Foundation. Used by permission of Tyndale House Publishers, Inc., Carol Stream, Illinois 60188. All rights reserved.

Scripture quotations marked MSG are taken from THE MESSAGE, copyright © 1993, 2002, 2018 by Eugene H. Peterson. Used by permission of NavPress. All rights reserved. Represented by Tyndale House Publishers, Inc.

Scripture quotations marked (AMP) are taken from the Amplified® Bible, Copyright © 2015 by The Lockman Foundation. Used by permission. www.lockman.org

Scripture quotations marked (ESV) are taken from the Holy Bible, English Standard Version (ESV®), copyright © 2001 by Crossway, a publishing ministry of Good News Publishers. Used by permission. All rights reserved.

Scripture quotations marked (NASB) are taken from the New American Standard Bible®, Copyright © 1960, 1962, 1963, 1968, 1971, 1972, 1973, 1975, 1977, 1995 by The Lockman Foundation. Used by permission. (www.lockman.org)

Scripture quotations marked (Phillips) are taken from The New Testament in Modern English by J. B. Phillips copyright © 1960, 1972 J. B. Phillips. Administered by The Archbishops' Council of the Church of England. Used by Permission.

Scripture quotations marked HCSB®, are taken from the Holman Christian Standard Bible®, Copyright © 1999, 2000, 2002, 2003, 2009 by Holman Bible Publishers. Used by permission. HCSB® is a federally registered trademark of Holman Bible Publishers.

Scripture quotations marked (TLB) are taken from The Living Bible copyright © 1971. Used by permission of Tyndale House Publishers, Carol Stream, Illinois 60188. All rights reserved.

Printed in the United States of America

First Printing — June 2021

Library of Congress Control Number: 2021934101

Contents

1

How Much Do We Really Love People Who Are Lost?

A few years ago, I was a professor at a small Christian liberal arts college in Minnesota. For a couple classes, I trained university students in Christian evangelism. On one occasion, we did a survey at the University of Minnesota where my students started conversations with other students and professors, and asked questions such as: "Do you believe truth is absolute or relative?"; "Do you believe there is a God?"; and "Can science answer everything?" I don't think anyone was converted on our first outreach, but I remember many students, who were not by nature outgoing, came back excited because of the meaningful conversations. My students were pleasantly surprised to see a professor change his mind on some of the answers regarding the nature of truth and the meaning of life, moving from someone who believed that truth was only relative to believing in an objective standard. On another occasion, our students went out to the Mall of America and talked with Somali Muslim young adults about Jesus. The experience was so positive that two of my students, Liam and Caleb, persisted in asking me to take them out again to share the gospel across the Twin Cities.

These two students both loved Jesus and wanted to make a difference. I finally agreed to organize a group of students and recruited another professor to go out and start spiritual conversations. It was a cold, snowy evening in downtown St. Paul, which I visited with Liam, Caleb, and a handful of other students and adults. Standing outside a bus stop, Caleb suggested we pray together as a group.

In my heart, I was hesitant, as I didn't want to draw attention to ourselves. But I thought it was great that Caleb was stepping out in faith, so we huddled beside the bus station and prayed out loud that God would use us as people walked by.

As we were praying, a lady said, "If you are praying, please say a prayer for me."

"Sure," I responded. "How can we pray for you?"

"I am an alcoholic," she said. "And I have been in and out of rehab. But Child Protection Services is going to take my baby if I don't quit drinking. I desperately need God's help." Then she started crying.

I have met many people with drinking problems, but few are willing to readily admit their addiction. As we prayed that God would do a miracle, tears ran down her face. We asked for the power of the Holy Spirit to fill her and take away her desire to drink. When we finished praying, she didn't ask for money. Our group thought it would be good to get to know her better and hear about her church experience, so we invited her to walk to McDonald's with us to grab a bite to eat. If Caleb hadn't suggested praying, she would never have talked with us.

As we walked to McDonald's, I started a conversation with a young, professional man named Anthony and asked him if he had a faith.

He told me, "Not really."

"Is there anything that interests you spiritually," I asked, "or do you have a church home?"

"Nope," he replied.

After asking a few more questions, I felt like I was getting nowhere with Anthony, so I continued on with our group. It seemed to me that Anthony was spiritually "cold" and not at all interested in having a spiritual conversation. I gave up and pleasantly thanked him for taking the time to talk with me.

But Liam was more persistent and wasn't going to allow an initial rejection to stop him. Liam spoke to Anthony and started asking bold questions: "If you were to die tonight, how sure are you on a scale from 1 to 10, you would go to heaven?"

I was thinking that his timing for these questions might not be the best since Anthony had already implied that he wasn't interested. Again, I started feeling a little embarrassed. Obviously, this man was not interested in the gospel, but Liam wouldn't stop talking.

"If you died tonight," Liam continued, "and God was to ask you 'Why should I let you into my kingdom?' what would you tell God?"

To keep things casual, I said, "Anthony, join us for McDonald's. I'm buying."

To my astonishment, he said, "Sure, I'll join."

As we entered the restaurant, I was busy with the group and making sure everyone was taken care of. After everyone had ordered, I was surprised to see Liam and Anthony praying together! Then they were laughing together. As I walked up, I could hear Liam talking clearly about the love and forgiveness of Jesus. Even though I was the professor and more well trained with degrees in religion, God chose to use Liam, a farm boy from North Dakota, in his obedience to lead Anthony closer to Jesus. While I had been feeling somewhat timid, young Liam's bold faith wouldn't be intimidated by an initial refusal. Of course, there had been times in my life when I was bold and took risks; but then other times, I needed encouragement to go out and spread the gospel.

Like my students, Liam and Caleb, I want you to be encouraged that God can use you to take risks and initiate conversations with people about Jesus. In this book, we are going to examine biblical examples, conversational strategies, and tips to help you grow in knowledge. Jesus said the greatest command is to "love the Lord your God with all your heart, soul, mind and strength" (Mark 12:30). This book will help equip you in wisdom as you are growing to "always be prepared to give an answer to anyone who asks you to give a reason for the hope you have" (1 Pet. 3:15). I will share effective conversational starters and ways to memorize and explain the gospel. Don't think you have to wait until you have all the answers and conversational tactics down to start talking about Jesus. You don't have to worry about becoming some preacher-type-person or developing a weird personality that's not your own. If you're willing to be used by God, he can take you—even with all your deficiencies—and make you an effective ambassador of good news. However, if you want to play it safe, or wait until you feel adequate enough, it's unlikely you will ever accomplish much for God's kingdom in this way.

We Are on a Rescue Mission

Do you remember watching the news when twelve teenage boys and their soccer coach were trapped in a long cave in the mountains of northern Thailand? On June 23, 2018, the young men parked their bicycles and dropped their backpacks and shoes outside the cavern and entered. Then it started to rain. Apparently, they had been there before and—though there were warning signs not to enter during the rainy season—they were determined to explore and touch a wall close to three miles into the cave. For the first half mile, the cavernous entrance with limestone rock formations had huge high ceilings; but deeper inside, according to local authorities, the passages narrowed into unsafe areas. The boys went into the cave before the rain and floodwaters increased, and then they were trapped for days.

Soon the whole world was aware of their peril, and everyone seemed willing to do anything to make sure these trapped young men would be rescued and set free. Day by day, the world anxiously awaited their rescue. Aid from the around the world joined the Thai Navy SEALs, realizing it had to be a carefully calculated attempt. Nearly a hundred divers, medical personnel, and support staff were engaged to rescue the young soccer players. Former Thai Navy SEAL Saman Kunan died in his operation to deliver oxygen tanks to the boys. Finally, the world celebrated as one by one the boys and their coach were saved, after days of wondering if there was any possible way they would be rescued.

The Bible tells us that we too were once lost and trapped in utter spiritual darkness, which is how the Bible portrays sin. Lost from wandering the wrong way, we had no hope of getting out of the darkness; but then God sent his Son, Jesus, on a rescue mission for us. The Bible tells us that God "rescued us from the dominion of darkness and brought us into the kingdom of the Son he loves" (Col. 1:13). After eighteen days of anxious watching, the whole world rejoiced as the last boy exited the flooded cave. Likewise, Jesus said there is a big celebration in heaven when one lost person repents (Luke 15:7).

One thing that was quite clear in this dramatic rescue mission of the trapped soccer boys is that it took planned preparation and extreme effort from the rescuers; it was no haphazard attempt. It was quite risky for the rescuers, and one even lost his life. In the same manner, if we who follow Christ want to join him in the "Great Rescue Commission," it can be no haphazard or careless effort. It's important that we adequately prepare ourselves to rescue others, to be willing to accept the risks, and even be prepared to lose ourselves in order to save others for the sake of Christ.

All around us, we have an opportunity to participate in God's Rescue Mission by sharing the good news of Jesus Christ. It's not always easy to share the gospel with people who don't believe the way we do; but we can better prepare ourselves, be persistent, and learn from those who have gone before us. Paul told a young man named Timothy to "proclaim the message; persist in it whether convenient or not" (2 Tim. 4:2 HCSB). Learning how to have "Jesus Conversations" effectively with people is a process, but the Lord can help ordinary people like us become "coworkers" with him.

It is an incredible thought to realize that there is a God in heaven who loves all *lost* people—including me! Sent on a radical rescue mission by his Father, Jesus Christ told us the reason why he came to earth: "For the Son of Man came to seek and to save *what was lost*" (Luke 19:10).

Have you heard of the term "Great Commission"? The Great Commission was the last charge Jesus gave his disciples before he ascended into heaven. With the full authority, Jesus commanded and commissioned his followers to go into all the world and make disciples, baptizing them and teaching them to obey all of his teaching. Matthew 28:18–20 is one of the most popular quotations of Jesus and has been commonly referred to as the Great Commission:

> Then Jesus came to them and said, "All authority in heaven and on earth has been given to me. Therefore go and make disciples of all nations, baptizing them in the name of the Father and of the Son and of the Holy Spirit, and teaching them to obey everything I have commanded you. And surely I am with you always, to the very end of the age."

The Great Commission, which was once common among Christians, has been talked about less frequently in churches. According to a 2017 Barna survey, only 51 percent of churchgoers said they know this term.[1] We as followers of Jesus are not saved by our works, but we will miss out on God's blessing of an abundant life if we're disobedient by not evangelizing the lost and making disciples.

Maybe at one point in your life, you had a passion to tell the world about Jesus. When we stand before Jesus one day and give an account for our lives, may we not be like the servant who was fearful of failure and did not take a risk to invest the gifts that his master had given him. Rather, may we be like the one who invested what was entrusted to him, so we too can hear our Lord say, "Well done, good and faithful servant. You have been faithful over a little, I will set you over much. Enter into the joy of your master" (Matt. 25:21). If you have lost the desire to be an obedient disciple maker, call out to Jesus and ask him, "Lord, here am I! Help me to see the lost and brokenness around me. Send me to evangelize and to make disciples!" When you pray, ask Jesus to use you immediately. Jesus said,

> "Don't you have a saying, 'It's still four months until harvest'? I tell you, open your eyes and look at the fields! They are ripe for harvest. Even now the one who reaps draws a wage and harvests

a crop for eternal life, so that the sower and the reaper may be glad together." (John 4:35–36)

Jesus also said to his disciples:

> "The harvest is plentiful, but the workers are few. Ask the Lord of the harvest, therefore, to send out workers into His harvest."
> (Matt. 9:37–38)

Right now, you and I can be workers by engaging in conversations with other people who do not believe the way we do. I wrote *Jesus Conversations* as a practical book about conversational evangelism, which I hope will guide you to engage people in a nonthreatening manner and to share the gospel more effectively.

Jesus Seeks after the Lost

Jesus didn't come to this world to help "good people get better" or to provide positive therapeutic teachings for all people to live by. The Bible says that, left to ourselves, none of us is good or righteous, but rather helpless, weak, and "lost" (Rom. 3–5). The theologian Karl Barth said, "Sin is man behaving naturally." We naturally tend to live selfish lives, looking after "number one," thinking little of God or other people. Therefore, we don't just need improvement; we need rescuing! We need to be changed—inside and out.

The word *lost* is a good description for people who don't know God, and that's how we all were! "Lost people" include outsiders, sinners, misguided religious people, the lonely, the isolated, the disobedient, the prideful, the forgotten, the failures, and the hopeless. The Bible describes the *lost* as those "who walk in darkness; who don't know the way" (Eph. 5:8) and those who choose to "do their own thing" (Isa. 53:6). We are lost, living apart from God, separated from him and from one another in our brokenness.

But here's the good news: Jesus loves these lost people, and that includes you and me! "Remember that at that time you were separate from Christ . . . without hope and without God in the world" (Eph. 2:12–13). The most famous verse in the Bible says, "God so *loved* the world that he gave his one and only Son" (John 3:16). This is the reason Jesus died a sacrificial death on a cross—to rescue those who are lost. Perhaps you've already discovered you were once lost, "but you were cleansed; you were made holy; you were made right with God by calling on the name of the Lord Jesus Christ and by the Spirit of our God" (1 Cor. 6:11 NLT). If so, I hope your interest in the spiritual welfare of others will grow.

Jesus Goes after the One Lost Sheep

In Luke 15, Jesus is described as the good shepherd who leaves ninety-nine sheep to pursue one lost lamb. I've been in a couple of megachurches on Sunday mornings where thousands of people, hands raised to Jesus, sing how he "chases me down, fights till I'm found, and leaves the ninety-nine." But after we worship Jesus for loving us when we were lost and taking the initiative to come to us, why is it that we go about our own lives and feel no passion or urgency to tell other lost people about him?

After church, what do we do? Perhaps we eat lunch, we hang out with our families and friends, we watch sports, we take naps, or we start planning our week. Although there's nothing wrong with enjoying our Sunday afternoons, do we *ever* actually tell lost people about Jesus? Do we forget what we sang in church? Or do we somehow think Jesus loves us more than other lost people? Of course, we don't. Do we think all that matters is that he chased us down and found us? No, we know quite well that God *so loved the world*.

Are we willing to leave our safe Christian circles at times to confidently and courageously engage a skeptic, a Mormon, a Muslim, an atheist, or an agnostic person? In an *Outreach* magazine survey, Christian readers who are primarily leaders were asked, "How many of you in the past six months have personally told somebody how to become a Christian?" Sixty-one percent of those surveyed said,

"Zero."[2] In my experience of speaking to many churches across the United States, I would estimate that only about 10 percent of Christians *ever* share the gospel with an unbeliever.

I wrote this book to encourage you to grow in a fourfold emphasis of becoming better initiators, asking good questions, making a case for the gospel, and answering tough questions. As we do all this, we need to be wholly dependent on God's power to love people.

There have been brilliant theologians who lost their focus of loving those who need God, and I know Christians who have a "great heart" but aren't growing intellectually. Jesus invited us to love him with *both* heart and mind; and to effectively love the lost, we must grow in both areas. We are seeing what is called the rise of the "nones" in America. Twenty-three percent of the U.S. population say their religion is "nothing in particular." This is a sharp contrast compared to ten years ago, when it was only 16 percent. Skeptics now represent one-quarter (25 percent) of all unchurched adults, and nearly one-third (31 percent) of skeptics have never attended a Christian church service. In other words, there are many people who don't take the Bible seriously. They think, "That's fine for you to attend your church, but it's not true for me."

In previous generations, evangelists such as Billy Graham would say, "The Bible says . . ." and non-Christians would respect its authority. Today, there is more skepticism toward it. But there has also been an acceleration of resources and interest in apologetics from great minds. While many Christians respect these brilliant intellectuals, most Christians, after hearing an inspiring message by one of them, feel unprepared to articulate their own spiritual convictions to someone who does not believe in the authority of Scripture. This book will be your guide in helping you grow so that you can confidently engage in conversations and your world for Christ.

Now, this book is not to beat you up with guilt if you aren't telling others about Jesus. If you have reservations or fears regarding talking about Jesus, you're not alone. I too have missed many opportunities to start conversations. Sometimes I'm too caught up with my own personal interests that I don't notice the person in the checkout line or during a business meeting. My current full-time job is medical sales, and every day I interact with physicians, medical assistants, and patients in the waiting room who are hurting and broken. How many times do I quickly pass by them so I can make the next sales call?

We could all look back at missed opportunities, *but starting today, God can use you in an extraordinary way to step out and show Christ's love by having a conversation about him.* Even though I've been walking with Christ for a couple of decades, I can become spiritually comfortable and apathetic and need to be reminded to use what God has given me to tell others about Jesus. Sometimes I believe I need to wait for the perfect opportunity or perhaps study more before I talk to a particular person. But when this happens, this means I'm forgetting how God uses ordinary (but willing) believers to lead lost people to Jesus.

Becoming a Conversational Evangelist in Everyday Life

Although Christianity is growing worldwide, in the United States, we are experiencing a decrease of evangelism. Out of the growing churches in America, very few are growing due to evangelism. Rather, most growth is due to transfer growth. In other words, people attend one church for a season because they like the singles ministry and community, but then switch to another church because they like the music or the preaching. Not all transfer-church growth is bad; but sometimes living in a culture of megachurches, we forget there are still many lost people who will never step foot in our churches.

Many of us go to worship services and gather with other believers in community or Bible studies. Occasionally, we engage in humanitarian or international trips, but very few of us feel comfortable articulating the truthfulness of Christ's death and resurrection to a peer outside the church who doesn't believe the way we do. These conversations become even more awkward in our culture when the discussion turns to ethical issues such as same-sex orientation, political issues, or "narrow-minded" religion.

Sometimes Christians feel intimidated by the objections of unbelievers who may look at us and say, "That's right for you, but not for me," or "That's just your opinion," or "I'm more of a person of science and not of faith." This book will provide questions, answers, and relational tips in overcoming these conversation stoppers.

In the past decade, I have given guest lectures to students at universities such as Yale, Duke, and the University of Virginia. I have also traveled to other countries and have spent a considerable amount of time with some of the world's leading defenders of the faith, while training Christians to share the gospel in culturally and religiously diverse cities like New York, Minneapolis, and Charlotte. But as I mentioned in the beginning of this chapter, I frequently need to be reminded by other Christians and the words of Scripture to forsake spiritual comfort and keep evangelizing, because our time on this earth is short. In Paul's last letter, he told a young leader named Timothy:

> This is why I remind you to fan into flames the spiritual gift God gave you when I laid my hands on you. For God has not given us a spirit of fear and timidity, but of power, love, and self-discipline. So never be ashamed to tell others about our Lord. (2 Tim. 1:6–8)

In this book, we will learn from the stories of ordinary people who proclaim the gospel without fear while visiting nursing homes, throwing parties, renting out a bar for open-minded skeptics, and talking to coworkers and teammates.

Are We Keeping the Good News to Ourselves?

In the days when Elisha was the prophet of Israel, there was a severe famine in which the people were starving to death. Oppressed by the Assyrians, the majority of God's people had lost all hope in God. Ben-Hadad, King of Syria, gathered his army to launch a large, full-scale attack against Samaria. The Assyrian army besieged Samaria and prevented all business and trade from entering or leaving the city. The siege strategy starved the people of Samaria. The famine was so severe that a donkey's head or dove droppings became so expensive that only the rich could afford them. Most of the people were hopeless and dying, except for four men who had leprosy.

> During this time, there were four men who had leprosy, a deadly disease. Then they said to each other, "Why are we sitting here until we die? Let us take a risk and go to the Syrian camp. Who knows? Maybe we can take them. But if they kill us, we are going to die anyway because we have leprosy." So the lepers arose at twilight to go to the camp of the Syrians. But when they came to the edge of the camp, there was no one there. For God had caused a miracle and had made the Syrian army hear the sounds of chariots and of horses, the sound of a great army, so that they had fled their own camp. They fled for their lives, leaving the camp as it was. And when these lepers came to the edge of the camp, they went into a tent and ate and drank, and they carried off silver and gold and clothing and went and hid them. Then they came back and entered another tent and carried off things from it and went and hid them. Just when they were hoarding as much as they could, they started realizing their own selfishness and said to one another, "We are not doing right. This day is a day of good news. If we are silent and wait until the morning light, punishment will overtake us. Now therefore come; let us go and tell the king's household." So they came and called to the gatekeepers of Israel and then the people went out and plundered the camp of the Syrians. (2 Kings 7)

What can we learn from this story? First, we learn the men had leprosy, which meant they were unclean and forced to sit outside the gate of their own people. We too were unclean, maybe not because of a disease, but because of impure sins, separated from God's favor. But while we were sinners, "Jesus suffered and died outside the city gates to make his people holy by means of his own blood" (Heb. 13:12). Our "spiritual leprosy" has been cleansed by the blood of Christ!

Second, these men were running out of time on earth. They asked, "Why sit here until we die?" With their little time, they wanted to make the most of every opportunity. What about us? Our time on this earth is also running out. Are we willing to start taking more risks?

Third, they saw the need to tell other people their good news. They refused to be selfish about the abandoned camp they had discovered, which meant that the enemy had fled. In fact, they said, "We're not doing *right*." Likewise, maybe we too have been silent, instead of telling others the good news we have discovered in Christ.

Looking back on my life, I am grateful for the times I took a risk to tell someone about Jesus. Rarely do I look back and think, "You know, I talked about Jesus too much." Most of the time, I do not talk about Jesus enough.

Be Willing to Step Out and Take a Risk

The restaurant in North Dallas was not too busy on Monday at 2pm. After picking up my food, I went to get my drink at the fountain. I couldn't help overhearing a group of men in their twenties talking loudly a few tables over. I was in a hurry, so I tried to ignore them. I sat down, said a quick silent prayer, and started to eat.

As I tried to enjoy my meal, their loud conversation turned sexually explicit and disturbing. Apparently, the previous night, they had been at a strip club, and they proceeded to degrade women and their bodies.

While the crude and obnoxious talk continued, I became annoyed. I was trying to eat peacefully and didn't want to be interrupted. *Should I say something to them?* I thought to myself. *How are they going to be receptive to some stranger confronting them?*

After all, I'm not this restaurant's manger. I don't want to come across as holier-than-thou. But then another thought came to my mind: *Dave, go talk to them.*

Whether it was the Holy Spirit or simply my conscience, I'm not sure. But I got up and walked toward the biggest and most vocal guy.

"Hi. Excuse me," I said. *How could I speak firmly, but also be calm and humble?* I looked him in the eye but kept my tone pleasant. "Hi. I wasn't trying to listen in but couldn't help overhearing part of your conversation. I'm very concerned about the way you were talking about a woman, and I don't appreciate it at all."

"Aw, I'm sorry, man," he replied. "I'll quiet down."

Instead of walking away, I sensed I needed to tell him about Jesus. "I'm Dave. What's your name?"

"Elon."

"Is it okay if I ask you a question?"

"Yeah." He seemed cool and open to have a conversation.

"Can I sit down?" I pulled up chair and sat down at his table with all of his friends. "Elon," I began, "do you believe there is a God?"

"Yeah, I guess so."

I noticed that the whole table of about eight men with tattoos, piercings, and bright jewelry started listening intently, including a young man who had a gold cross around his neck.

"Me too. You're right. There is a God, and the reason I sat down is that he wanted me to tell you that he loves you very much. He also loves the woman, or women, you were talking about. The words I heard spoken about her were degrading and disrespectful. The Bible says that God is righteous and holy. That means he is so perfect that he is separate from any sin. You've heard the word *sin*, right?"

"Yes," Elon replied.

"Sin is any thought, word, or action we do that isn't pleasing to God and is rebellious toward him. Elon, I've committed a lot of sins in my life. Have you ever heard of the Ten Commandments?"

"Yeah."

"Do you know any of the Ten Commandments?"

"Um, yeah." After a pause, Elon smiled. "I forgot."

The guy with the cross necklace spoke up, "Thou shalt not murder."

"Exactly! That's a famous commandment. Now, I'm guessing that no one in this room has ever *murdered* someone. But Jesus said that if you have hatred in your heart, you have committed murder in your heart. I've certainly had evil thoughts in my heart. Have you?"

Elon nodded his head.

I continued, "Likewise, Jesus said that if you've ever lusted toward a woman, you've committed adultery in your heart. Based on God's commands, if you were to stand before God on the day of judgment, do you think you would be guilty or innocent?"

Elon didn't hesitate. "Guilty."

"If you're guilty before a Holy God, then are you going to heaven or hell?"

"I'm not sure. Hell, I guess."

"Elon, hell is real. Jesus spoke of a literal place of torment called hell, but the Bible tells us that 'God loved the world so much, that he gave his one and only Son that whoever believes in him shall not perish but have everlasting life.'"

I told him how there was a time when I was dependent on my parent's faith; and if you had asked me what was most important, I would have said basketball. Yet, when I was seventeen, a man challenged me to make a decision to fully surrender to Christ's Lordship.

Then I sensed the Holy Spirit encouraging me to act boldly. "Elon, are you willing to surrender and humble yourself right now and place your trust in Jesus and receive his salvation for the forgiveness of sins?"

He paused and then said, "Nah, I'm not ready for that. No, I don't want to do that."

I felt a sense of disappointment and embarrassment. *Was this an overzealous mistake of me going Billy Graham on these guys, calling out their sin, and asking them to trust Jesus?* I suppressed my doubts and asked another question: "What about anybody else at this table?

Right now, I want to invite anybody at this table to humble himself before God and each other and receive Christ as Lord of your life. Who wants to surrender his faith to Jesus right now?"

A man and the end of the table raised his hand. "I do."

"What's your name?" I asked.

"I'm Jamir."

I then asked Jamir if he wanted to say of prayer of surrender and faith in Jesus, trusting in his death and resurrection for the forgiveness of sins. After we prayed together out loud, with him repeating after me, I talked to him about the importance of following Jesus, turning away from sin, and knowing Christ more deeply through prayer, Bible reading, and being part of church where he could grow closer to God along with other people.

The whole group suddenly became friendly and started asking more questions about the faith. I invited all of them to my church, which had a gathering for young singles the following evening. But they told me they were just passing through on their way to another city. They were a rap group that had their first single as a top 100 song on iTunes, and they had to leave for a concert in another city.

As far as I know, Jamir didn't quit the rap group, and I have no idea how he is doing these days. *Was Jamir sincere when he prayed?* While I can't be sure, I do know that sometimes God uses us when we step out in faith to start a conversation about the hope we have in Jesus Christ. It may not be just for the person we originally talk to; it could be someone else close by and eager to receive the good news.

Now, perhaps you're thinking what a friend told me: "I could never just walk up to a stranger and tell them about Jesus. I wouldn't even know what to say." There was a time when I wouldn't have known this either.

A Big Turning Point in My Life

I grew up in a Christian family, but rarely did I feel comfortable talking about Jesus. In fact, I was scared to talk about Jesus. I could engage in conversations about noncontroversial subjects or things I was interested in, like sports. But Jesus? With strangers? With unbelievers? Then several events happened that changed my perspective. Here is one significant turning point in my life.

When I was a junior in high school, I went to a Christian evangelistic youth event at a basketball arena in the state of Virginia. The speaker spoke loudly to the stadium filled with teenagers, asking us, "Are you unashamed of Jesus?"

Up until that point in my life, I had frequently doubted my salvation. I prayed to receive Christ as a little child because I knew I was a sinner, but I was often afraid and even sometimes *ashamed* of talking about the name of Jesus publicly. Truthfully, even though I believed in Jesus so I wouldn't go to an eternal hell, there were things that were more important to me than Jesus. *God, are you really first? Am I saved?* I prayed silently. One of those things I had put above God was basketball. I loved playing ball. I had grown to the height of six feet six inches tall and was dreaming of becoming a Division One basketball player.

Now don't get me wrong, there is nothing sinful about basketball, but I was putting it above God. You could have asked me for any statistic about the greatest players and teams in both college and professional sports, and I would have unashamedly shared details along with my analysis and opinions about the sport. But ask me about Jesus, and I would have become awkward.

The evangelist challenged us. "Is Jesus *Lord* of your life? *Lord* means that he is supreme. He's #1. He's your Savior and you're unashamed of him. Jesus said, 'If anyone is ashamed of me and my words in this adulterous and sinful generation, the Son of Man will be ashamed of them when he comes in his Father's glory with the holy angels'" (Mark 8:38). He quoted Jesus again, "Whoever confesses me before men, I will also confess him before my Father in heaven, but whoever denies me before men, I will also deny him before My Father in heaven" (Matt. 10:32–33).

As the evangelist was preaching, my heart started pounding, and I thought to myself, *Why am I so afraid to confess the name of Jesus before other people?*

Then he said, "If you're not sure if you are truly saved, tonight is the night to put a stake in the ground and make a decision to surrender to Jesus, the one who died and rose again for the forgiveness of sins. So right now, in this stadium, I am going to ask you to stand up unashamed and at the top of your lungs tell Jesus, 'I am yours, Lord!'"

I heard a couple voices from across the stadium yell, "I AM YOURS!"

With my heart still pounding, I stood up and raised my voice to Jesus: "I AM YOURS, LORD!"

The evangelist asked us to come forward for prayer, and though I'm not emotional, I started crying. From that point on, I quit regularly doubting my salvation and my conversations about Jesus started coming naturally.

The Bible says, "God saved you by his grace when you believed. And you can't take credit for this; it is a gift from God" (Eph. 2:8 NLT). Although I had believed at a young age, because of my doubts, it was important for me to publicly and boldly confess Jesus now in front of my peers.

Have you ever confidently told other people that Jesus Christ is the Lord of your life and that he has changed everything? Before you start telling people about Jesus, however, examine your own relationship with Christ. Is he truly Lord of your life? Have you placed your trust in him alone? "Examine yourselves to see whether you are in the faith; test yourselves. Do you not realize that Christ Jesus is in you—unless, of course, you fail the test?" (2 Cor. 13:5). Call out to the Lord right now if you're unsure of where you stand. Then tell other people what he has done.

The apostle Paul declared, "For I am not ashamed of the Gospel, because it is the power of God for the salvation of everyone who believes, for the Jew first and also for the Gentile" (Rom. 1:16). I want to encourage you to grow in becoming unashamed of Jesus. For some people it may happen immediately; for others, they may not feel bold, but they can take a simple step of obedience, one move at a time. That step of obedience may mean starting a conversation with a stranger, classmate, neighbor, or coworker.

How can we become unashamed of Jesus if we're not willing to initiate conversations with those around us who don't believe the way we do? Let's explore how to start conversations and how God can use us right now to talk to someone about Jesus.

2

THE HOLY SPIRIT CAN USE YOU

Have you ever heard of a man named Edward Kimball? Edward was a dry goods salesman in Boston and a faithful Sunday school teacher for many years. Although somewhat timid about sharing his faith, one day in April 1855 he felt compelled to talk to one of his eighteen-year-old Sunday school students about his soul.

On the way to the shoe store where the young man was employed, Edward started to question the idea of this visit, especially during working hours. He wondered if such a conversation might be embarrassing for the young man in front of his fellow workers. He walked past the entrance a couple times, pondering if he should take such a bold initiative. Finally, Edward decided "to have it over at once" and went in to make what he later thought was "a weak plea" for the young man to come to Christ.

Despite his lack of eloquence, Edward Kimball had a compassionate heart and tears in his eyes as he talked about God's love. In those few minutes, in the back of this Boston shoe store, young Dwight L. Moody surrendered his life to Jesus Christ. Moody would become America's best-known evangelist in the nineteenth century, preaching to more people than ever before in history. For years, D. L. Moody filled arenas, preaching to crowds of 60,000 in one day. It's estimated that a million people trusted in Christ because of the preaching of this evangelist. But while many people have heard of D. L. Moody, few have ever heard of Edward Kimball.

Whenever we consider whether or not we should share our Christian convictions to someone, we often feel inadequate, thinking that someone else could do a better job. Yet God chooses ordinary people to display his glory. The Bible and church history are full of examples of ordinary people who were available and used by God in extraordinary ways. God can certainly use you!

Think of this: Maybe you have a non-Christian classmate, neighbor, relative, or fellow worker. You may be *the only Christian on earth* that person knows (this thought sobers me when I think about it). If you're wondering if you can be an adequate witness to the good news for this person, be assured that *God can use you!* God frequently chooses those who seem the least likely to do the work of personal evangelism. This only leads to him being glorified that much more!

Several years ago, I became concerned about the abortions taking place a few miles from my neighborhood in North Dallas. When Dr. Curtis Boyd opened the late-term abortion facility, called the Southwestern Women's Surgery Center, he was asked on the local Dallas news, "Are you killing?" his response was, "Am I killing? Yes, I am. I know that." He then said, "I am an ordained Baptist minister." He described how after he killed the baby, he prayed that God would receive the child's soul.

I knew this was demonic deception as Satan has always hated babies. During the time of Moses' birth, Satan inspired Pharaoh to command the Hebrews to kill their baby boys. During the time of Jesus' birth, Herod ordered the slaughter of boys two years and under in Bethlehem. And since the 1973 *Roe v. Wade* decision legalizing abortion, Americans have killed over sixty million babies!

I ask my pro-life friend Carmen Pate how I could get involved, especially as a man. I'm obviously not a counselor or a politician, so other than making posts on Facebook, I asked her if she knew what I could do to help. "Yes!" she said. "You can pray." She then told me about 40 Days for Life, a ministry that focused on having a prayerful presence outside abortion facilities across the country. Carmen said she would love for me to become involved with them. At first, she wanted me to serve on the ministry's national board, but I wanted to begin with praying. So, I started praying outside abortion centers in Texas, waiting for the opportunity to share a few words of hope to young couples who were preparing to have their child killed.

Many times, it was just me and a few elderly Catholic ladies praying. I felt inadequate, awkward, and overwhelmed by the task. Every few minutes, I saw women walk up to the facility, sometimes accompanied by a boyfriend or husband. I often sensed an evil presence, and yet I felt there was nothing I could do.

Despite my feelings of doubt, however, the Lord used me. The apostle John wrote, "Greater is he who is in you, then he who is in the world" (1 John 4:4), which encouraged me to invite friends to pray with me outside the building.

I remember one time talking to a young woman in the parking lot. "Hi," I said. "We would love to help you. Do you mind me asking, what brings you here today?"

"You know. . ." She paused and looked down as she said to me, "I'm here for an abortion."

I responded, "This is such an important decision and before you make it, would you consider going to the Pregnancy Center across the street where you can get a free sonogram?"

"I suppose," she replied.

"I'm Dave, by the way. What's your name?"

"I'm Glory."

"Glory, that's a Christian name! Are you religious or spiritual?"

"Yes, I am listening to gospel music right now."

I wanted to get to know her, but I also wanted to stall time because I knew Glory was about to have her unborn child killed. Not sure what to say, I just spoke up in faith. "Well, Glory, since you are a believer and I know you're making a very important decision, would it be okay if I read you the story about Mary, when she discovered she was in her early pregnancy with baby Jesus?" I then read her the story from Luke's Gospel: "When Elizabeth heard Mary's greeting, the *baby* [John the Baptist] leaped in her womb" (Luke 1:41–42). I also read to her the Gospel Christmas story and talked about the celebration between the babies of John the Baptist and Jesus, and how God helped Elizabeth and Mary, and that he was going to do the same with her.

"Glory, is there someone in your family or church who loves you that you can talk to about this pregnancy? Because with a name like Glory, I'm guessing somebody in your family has faith in the Lord." She started crying and said, "My grandmother. I can talk to her."

I asked Glory if I could pray with her. As I held her hand, I prayed that the Holy Spirit would intervene and show her that just as he was present with Mary in her pregnancy, he was already with Glory, giving her the strength to obey him and carry this child. I prayed out loud for Jesus to protect the little baby inside her womb and recited Psalm 139 about her baby already being "fearfully and wonderfully made."

After that, Glory left without going into the abortion facility. I never talked to her again, so I don't know what she ended up choosing to do. All I knew was that I needed to say *something*.

As a man, I could have bought into the lies I've heard from so many about how it's better for men to stay out of the pro-life movement, because they can't get pregnant. This is an outright lie from Satan. God can use men to make a difference in the pro-life movement. We all know every pregnancy involves a mother *and a father*. We also know that seven *men* on the Supreme Court decided the horrible decision of *Roe v. Wade*, which made abortion legal in the United States. What I said to Glory was true, whether I was male or female, a professional counselor or a volunteer willing to pray on the sidewalk outside of the abortion facility.

Maybe you feel inadequate. Regardless of your situation, though, *God can use you* to bring the good news of Jesus to others. When the apostle Paul wrote to the church at Corinth, not all of them were impressed with his public speaking and some preferred to hear a more eloquent preacher named Apollos. Paul, however, encouraged them not to place too much confidence in skillful communication but rather to trust in the power of the gospel:

Brothers, think of what you were when you were called. Not many of you were wise by human standards; not many were influential; not many were of noble birth. But God chose the foolish things of the world to shame the wise; God chose the weak things of the world to shame the strong. (1 Cor. 1:26–27)

Although you may feel you're not the most prepared or qualified person to talk about Jesus, God can help you grow into maturity and sharpen your skills. *He can use you right now* despite any imperfections in your presentation of his truth.

What Is an Evangelist?

The Greek word for "evangelist" was used in the ancient world to describe a messenger delivering good news of a general's victory. A couple of hundred years later, the writers of the New Testament also used it to describe someone who brought the good news about salvation offered through Christ's death and resurrection. The term "good news," used seventy-two times in the New Testament, is translated as "gospel."

In the book of Acts 6, we learn about a man named Philip who was called an "evangelist" or "one proclaiming good news." When a conflict arose in the early church about how the Hellenistic Jewish widows were being overlooked in food distribution, the apostles asked "the brothers to choose seven men" from among them, who were "known to be full of the Spirit and wisdom" (Acts 6:3). Philip was one of these godly and wise men asked to take care of the needs of the church, which allowed the apostles to devote themselves to prayer and to preaching the word.

After taking care of these seemingly ordinary ministry matters, the Lord sent Philip out on the road.

[Philip] started out, and he met the treasurer of Ethiopia, a eunuch of great authority under the Kandake, the queen of

Ethiopia. The eunuch had gone to Jerusalem to worship, and he was now returning. Seated in his carriage, he was reading aloud from the book of the prophet Isaiah.

The Holy Spirit said to Philip, "Go over and walk along beside the carriage."

Philip ran over and heard the man reading from the prophet Isaiah. Philip asked, "Do you understand what you are reading?"

The man replied, "How can I, unless someone instructs me?" And he urged Philip to come up into the carriage and sit with him.

The passage of Scripture he had been reading was this:

"He was led like a sheep to the slaughter. And as a lamb is silent before the shearers, he did not open his mouth. He was humiliated and received no justice. Who can speak of his descendants? For his life was taken from the earth" [Isa. 53:7–8].

The eunuch asked Philip, "Tell me, was the prophet talking about himself or someone else?" So, beginning with this same Scripture, Philip told him the Good News about Jesus.

As they rode along, they came to some water, and the eunuch said, "Look! There's some water! Why can't I be baptized?" He ordered the carriage to stop, and they went down into the water, and Philip baptized him. (Acts 8:27–38 NLT)

Normally, we think of an evangelist as someone like Billy Graham, who preached to millions and packed-out stadiums in the twentieth century. While he was certainly considered one of the greatest evangelists, not every evangelist is a full-time professional filling up stadiums.

What do we notice about Philip? First, he was willing to serve the widows in his church so the apostles could devote themselves to preaching and prayer. Just as Philip was faithful in ordinary ways,

God also used him in *extra*ordinary ways. As Paul says, an evangelist is someone who is always prepared "in season and out of season" (2 Tim. 2:4). As a student of the Scriptures, Philip was able to discuss the very passage the Ethiopian man asked him about.

Philip can be a reminder to us that an evangelist can be someone who works a regular job and not just a well-known preacher. Philip was also a faithful father in his home and is later mentioned in the book of Acts as having four daughters who "prophesied" (Acts 21:8).

Flexible to Work and to Evangelize

Sometimes an evangelist needs to be flexible—willing to work as well as share the gospel with others. Paul said he had every right to earn a living from preaching the gospel because the Lord had commanded that the "laborer is worthy of his wages" (1 Cor. 9:14). But when the church was unable to help Paul out financially, he was willing to earn his bread by going back to making tents, which was a good example to believers young in their faith (e.g., Acts 18:1–3). Currently, I work in medical sales and have the opportunity to be around unbelievers on a daily basis. This is where I need to be flexible. As I go about my business, I want to be ready for God to use me in evangelism whenever he leads me.

Likewise, in your job, you're probably surrounded by people who aren't connected to a church. This means that a pastor can't just walk into your workspace and spread the good word. In my role, I have access to physicians throughout Dallas, but my pastor doesn't. Your pastor is frequently surrounded by believers, working on sermons, equipping church staff, and counseling believers, while you have an opportunity to be surrounded by people who are lost!

We also learn from Philip's life that God uses anyone in evangelism. As we saw in Acts 21:8–9, Philip had four unmarried daughters who prophesied. So, we also see that someone who is doing the work of an evangelist can be single or married. Although they were not apostles like Peter and Paul, they certainly proclaimed the good news of Jesus, allowing their singleness to be used by the Lord. I do have some married friends who travel a lot, but traveling can be pretty hard for some families. In my singleness, it's been easy for me to travel and proclaim the gospel to others in Africa, Costa Rica, Russia, Poland, Mexico, the Netherlands, Germany, Israel, England, France, and Canada—which would have been much more difficult if I had a family. But whether you're single or married, male or female, Jesus can use you to evangelize.

Earlier in this chapter, I mentioned how God used me to speak to a woman who was considering an abortion. I said to myself, "I'm a man and not a counselor, so what difference can I make with a young woman who is pregnant?" Like me, you may think someone else could be better in sharing the gospel. Well, some people think that Jesus could have done "better" than to start with the twelve men he chose. But through the Holy Spirit's power, these ordinary "unqualified" men turned the world upside down by spreading Jesus' message!

Let's now explore the most common excuses why Christians don't share the good news of Jesus and discover how God can help us overcome each of these.

Excuses for Not Sharing the Good News

Excuse #1: "What If I'm Rejected?"

When you talk to someone about Jesus, there is always the possibility of rejection. In other areas of life, we realize that being rejected or receiving a no is not always a loss. So why are we so scared of being rejected for Christ's sake? Many guys have been rejected by a girl, but they later met someone more suitable. A young woman named Emily Cavanaugh broke off her engagement with a young Billy Graham at Florida Bible Institute because "she wanted to marry a man who was going to amount to something." An article in *Time* magazine said:

The disappointment planted in Graham a determination to prove her wrong; it ripened alongside his commitment to discerning, and obeying, God's will. He would practice sermons aloud in old sheds or in a canoe in the middle of a lake. He ate a quarter-pound of butter a day to try to spread some bulk across his lanky frame, and he worked on his gestures and facial expressions as he traveled to tiny churches or declaimed outside saloons frequented by drunkards and prostitutes, sharing the Gospel.[1]

For Billy, romantic rejection was not the end of the story. Not only would he work hard to become better at his preaching, but he later transferred to Wheaton College where he would meet the love of his life, Ruth Bell. They were married for sixty-four years when she died in 2007. Many people have similar stories, so we know that rejection in romantic relationships is not always the end of the story. The greatest love story, however, is the gospel. If you consistently proclaim the gospel, you will indeed be rejected on many occasions.

Numerous professionals face rejection from time to time. For example, teachers can be frustrated with students who seemed disengaged; but the teacher who persists with those students may eventually change their attitude and help them grow into maturity. Writers may be rejected by a hundred publishers until they finally find success. If a patient doesn't respond to a certain treatment, this doesn't mean the doctor will give up practicing medicine. The most obvious example is salespeople. Part of their job necessarily involves rejection, but they take it with poise.

If we share our faith at all, we can expect to be rejected, and it is often the hardest when it comes from a close friend or a relative. Young adults, you especially must choose who will be most important in your life—friends or Jesus? But consider this: If your best friend had cancer and you had the cure, wouldn't you share it? In this case, you have the cure for reconciling them with their Creator, which is a relationship with Jesus Christ. If you truly loved your friend, why would you hold back the most wonderful gift you could ever give—the gift of life?

We should never fear rejection for the sake of Christ. In fact, Jesus said you are blessed and receive true happiness *when you are rejected* because of him.

> "Blessed are you when men hate you, when they exclude you and insult you and reject your name as evil, because of the Son of Man. Rejoice in that day and leap for joy, because great is your reward in heaven. For that is how their fathers treated the prophets. . . . Woe to you when all men speak well of you."
>
> (Luke 6:22–26)

Evangelist Mark Cahill says, "Do you realize that when you get rejected in the name of Jesus, God has rewards waiting in Heaven that will make any earthly reward seem like chump change? That is truly amazing."[2] No matter the results, Cahill says you win!

First, if you share the gospel with an unbeliever, and they receive it, then you win! Second, perhaps the person you're talking to is a backslidden believer. God may use you to convict them when they see your boldness and decide to follow Jesus again. "Whoever turns a sinner from the error of their way will save them from death and cover over a multitude of sins" (James 5:20).

Third, maybe the person is not ready to receive Christ or fully embrace your ideas, but God may be using you to "plant a seed." God may be using you as the one to plant an idea in their mind to make them reconsider their current position. In 1 Corinthians, Paul wrote, "I planted the seed, Apollos watered it, but God has been making it grow." In God's eyes, that's a win!

The fourth possibility is that you could be rejected. With that rejection, you could lose a friend or even be insulted. In the world's eyes, this may seem like a loss, but it's not. It's a win! Jesus said that you are "blessed" or "happy" when people insult you or persecute you because of him (Matt. 5:11–12). I like the Eugene Peterson translation that says,

"Count yourselves blessed every time people put you down or throw you out or speak lies about you to discredit me. What it means is that the truth is too close for comfort and they are uncomfortable. You can be glad when that happens—give a cheer, even!—for though they don't like it, *I* do! And all heaven applauds. And know that you are in good company. My prophets and witnesses have always gotten into this kind of trouble."

(Matt. 5:11–12 The Message)

Excuse #2: *"Evangelism Is Wrong"*

Some professing Christians think evangelism is wrong. According to Barna research released in 2019, millennials are unsure about the actual practice of evangelism. Almost half of millennials (47 percent) agree at least somewhat that it's wrong to share one's personal beliefs with someone of a different faith in hopes they will one day share the same faith.[3] This is compared to a little over one-quarter of Gen X (27 percent), and one in five boomers (19 percent) and elders (20 percent). Among Generation Z (born between 1999 and 2005), atheism has doubled.

I saw a video featuring Penn Jillette, from the famous illusionist duo Penn & Teller. Penn is an outspoken atheist who doesn't believe that Christianity is true. When a man came to him after a show, gave him a Bible, and tried to convert him, Penn shared this story on a YouTube video.[4] Here is a portion of Penn's response to that encounter:

The man said, "I'm a businessman. I'm sane; I'm not crazy." And he looked me right in the eye and did all this. And it was really wonderful. I believe he knew that I was an atheist.

But he was not defensive, and he looked me right in the eyes and he was truly complimentary. It did not seem like empty flattery. He was really kind, and nice, and sane, and looked me in the eyes and talked to me. Then he gave me this Bible.

I've always said I don't respect people who don't try to convert me. I don't respect that at all. If you believe that there's a

heaven and a hell, and people could be going to hell or not getting eternal life, and you think that it's not really worth telling
them this because it would make it socially awkward—and atheists who think people should not try to convert you and who
say just leave me alone and keep your religion to yourself—*how
much do you have to hate somebody to not try to convert them?
How much do you have to hate somebody to believe everlasting
life is possible and not tell them that?*

I mean, if I believed, beyond the shadow of a doubt, that a
truck was coming at you, and you didn't believe that truck was
bearing down on you, there is a certain point where I tackle
you. And this is more important than that.

How amazing is this? Here a self-confessed atheist understands
that believing in heaven and hell should move Christians to evangelize. What made the difference with this man witnessing to Penn? He
loved him and had sincere concern for him. Our love and boldness
can indeed make a difference.

*Excuse #3: "I Don't Want to Be Seen as an Overzealous Street
Preacher"*

Don't worry; you probably won't. By the way, do you really
know any preachers who are too forceful or yell at people from the
street corner? I don't. Once in a rare while, we'll see some weirdo
on YouTube making an embarrassment of the gospel as he yells
out absurdities, but again this is one of the great myths people have
brought against evangelism. Living in Dallas, I have rarely seen
preachers on street corners with a megaphone. I did hear a young
man once who was preaching. He had friends with him and they
gave out water bottles as he proclaimed the gospel. He seemed to
be respected by a lot of the homeless people near the bus stop. So,
don't worry about being a "pushy preacher." And if you are pushing
people toward the truth, you're in company with John the Baptist,
Paul, and Jesus himself.

Sometimes we don't want to be known as radical, religious people or fanatics, but Jesus said we must confess his name before people and not be ashamed of our faith (Matt. 10:32; Mark 8:38). Honestly, most of us probably have never experienced someone calling us "narrow-minded" or a "bigot" for our faith in Jesus or obedience to the Bible. Although we don't seek conflict for conflict's sake, the gospel is offensive because it says that we are sinners who need to repent and trust in Jesus alone for the forgiveness of sins. Paul wrote, "I'm not trying to win the approval of people, but of God. If pleasing people were my goal, I would not be Christ's servant" (Gal. 1:10).

In May 2013, Vatican spokesman Archbishop Sivano Maria Tomassi addressed the United Nations Human Rights Council, saying, "Credible research has reached the shocking conclusion that an estimate of more than 100,000 Christians are violently killed because of some relation to their faith every year."[5] That's a lot of people all around the world who are dying because of their belief in Jesus. In America, however, we often fail to talk about Jesus. Not because of death threats, but because we fear what other people may think.

Excuse #4: "Evangelism Is Not My Gift"

In Romans 12:7, Paul writes, "If your gift is serving, serve them well." But let's suppose I told you that serving isn't my gift and that I won't serve my church, my family, or other believers. You would rightfully think that I'm selfish! Living in Texas, I wish I had the ability of Chip Gaines of the reality show *Fixer-Upper* to remodel an old building and make it look beautiful. But just because I'm not as gifted as Chip in handiwork, this doesn't mean I shouldn't pick up a paint brush on occasion to serve those less fortunate in West Dallas. Maybe you're not a gifted preacher or public speaker, but God can use you in one-on-one conversations with people your pastor may never meet.

I don't think I'm especially gifted with teaching children, but our church was recently in need of volunteers. So, I signed up to serve with the kindergarten students. Tara, who leads the kindergarten ministry at my church, immediately found a task for me to do. Because I'm six feet seven inches tall, she asked me to dress up like Goliath and take a few marshmallows to the head. The kids got kick out of it when I hit the ground.

Most of us would never say, "Giving is not my gift, so I'm not going to tithe to my church or tip the waitress." Then why would we use our lack of gifting in evangelism as an excuse not to tell someone in a one-on-one conversation about the One who means the most to us? You may not feel that evangelism is your primary gift, but the Holy Spirit can use you because of your willingness to love and serve him. In Paul's final letter, he instructs Timothy (who was probably more a pastor than an evangelist) to "do the work of an evangelist" (2 Tim. 4:5). This is a word for each of us. There will be occasions when each of us, despite our limitations or hesitations, can do evangelistic work.

The great evangelist of the nineteenth century, D. L. Moody, said, "I am only one, but I am one. I cannot do everything, but I can do something. What I can do, I ought to do. What I ought to do, by the grace of God, I will do."[6] Talking to others about Jesus may not be your best gift, but surely there is *one* person you can talk to about Jesus.

Excuse #5: "I Just Want to Live the Gospel"

We should certainly watch our lives. Paul wrote to Timothy, "Watch your life and doctrine closely" (1 Tim. 4:16). You may have heard someone quote Saint Francis of Assisi as saying, "Preach the gospel and when necessary use words." (It's unlikely he actually said this; it was attributed to him years later, and many historians question its origin.) But who among us has ever come to Christ without someone proclaiming the gospel message to us? We must use words to proclaim the message of Christ's salvation. As Paul writes, "How can they believe in him if they have never heard about him? And how can they hear about him *unless someone tells them*?"

(Rom. 10:14 NLT; my italics). Yes, we should live the gospel in our obedience to it, but we *must proclaim* the gospel using words. Part of living the gospel means obeying Jesus' Great Commission to *go and tell* other people his good news (Matt. 28:19–20).

Excuse #6: "I Shouldn't Try to Argue People into the Kingdom; that's the Holy Spirit's Job"

Some Christians want to avoid any controversy or conflict because they think it's contrary to the work of the Holy Spirit. For example, if there is an argument between a Mormon and a Christian, they can become extremely uncomfortable and want to seek peace without any confrontation. But this attitude of avoiding disagreement and confrontation is contrary to what we see in the Gospels. Yes, of course, it's true we don't want to be argumentative or rude. We should start with an area of common ground and avoid foolish arguments and quarrels. As we see in the New Testament, sound argument, disagreement, and persuasion are not in conflict with the Holy Spirit. By arguing, we do not mean high-pitched emotional yelling; we mean persuasion, which sometimes can remove ignorance or objections toward the gospel we're presenting.

Throughout the book of Acts, we see how the Holy Spirit uses the human element as believers persuade others of the gospel. For example, when Paul is in Thessalonica, Luke records him as "reasoning with them from the Scriptures, explaining and proving that the Christ had to suffer and rise from the dead" (Acts 17:3). Jude says, "Contend for the faith" (Jude 3); and Paul wrote, "We destroy arguments and every pretension that sets it up against the knowledge of Christ" (2 Cor. 10:5). While many people have come to faith in Jesus because someone argued them into the kingdom, we know that this was never apart from the saving work of the Holy Spirit. The Holy Spirit works through arguments and our preaching to bring people to the saving grace of the Lord. Jesus has invited us to fulfill this Great Commission, but he also said, "Apart from me, you can do nothing" (John 15:5).

So, what is our role, and what is the Holy Spirit's role? Well, the Holy Spirit uses our words as tools. While our proclamation and explanation of the gospel can convince someone *that* the gospel is true, it is the Holy Spirit who moves their heart to believe *in* the gospel for salvation. Our proclamation of the good news is, so to speak, to lead the "horse" to water, but the Holy Spirit is the one who will use our proclamation to make the "horse" drink. In other words, our proclamation and arguments help the person to *perceive* the truth in their mind, while the Holy Spirit uses our words to change hearts to *receive* the truth.

Excuse #7: "I Don't Know Enough"

You may know more than you think you do. That's why it's important to just *go* and *grow as you go*. Remember, when Jesus called us, most of us were not the smartest or the most capable by the world's standards. As we walk with Jesus—loving him with our hearts and minds, and sharing with unbelievers what he has done for us—we will grow in our knowledge and understand more spiritual matters. But you don't wait until you have all the answers to start sharing the good news. The Samaritan woman who met Jesus at a well had five husbands, and the man she was currently living with wasn't her husband. But when she met Jesus, she was changed immediately. She left her water jar, went to the town, and started telling everyone, "Come, see a man who told me everything I ever did. Could this be the Messiah?" (John 4:29).

She didn't have all her theology correct at this point, but she started with what she did know. As a result of her enthusiasm, the townspeople went out to meet Jesus.

> Many of the Samaritans from that town believed in him because of the woman's testimony, "He told me everything I ever did." So when the Samaritans came to him, they urged him to stay with them, and he stayed two days. And because of his words many more became believers. (John 4:40–41)

Some of my friends were saved at a midweek gathering for singles at my church in Dallas, because a friend or coworker (who were also new in their faith) invited them to "come and see." Similarly, you can start with what you know and share that with others.

Peter and John were uneducated, ordinary fishermen when Jesus first called them; but after Jesus returned to heaven, they continued to grow in their knowledge and wisdom. This process took quite some time, even after they had spent three years learning from the greatest teacher of all time. If you read their writings, even though they're not as articulate as Paul or the writer of Hebrews, they were both intelligent and accurate in their explanation of Christ. We know they didn't start that way. They spent years studying, traveling, and spending time evangelizing in Jewish synagogues, and also speaking the gospel to skeptics in Rome and Greece. John, who died as an old man on the island of Patmos in Greece, was able to reference the Greek philosophers and make the case that Jesus was the *Logos*, the Word, the source of all wisdom who was divine and who had created the world. Although Peter said some of the letters of "our beloved brother Paul" were "hard to understand," Peter knew the importance of loving Jesus with our minds. He said, "Honor Christ the Lord as Holy, always be prepared to give an answer to everyone who asks you to give a reason for the hope that you have but do this with gentleness and respect" (1 Pet. 3:15).

Excuse #8: "I'm Too Busy"

Everybody is busy, but Jesus told us, "What good is it if you gain the entire world, yet forfeit your soul?" (Matt. 16:26). The value of one's soul is priceless, and we should do our best to *make time* to win souls to Jesus. Isn't it interesting that even though Jesus had more responsibility than any person who ever lived, he made time for people? What if we allowed the overflow of Jesus to be poured out to everyone we already interact with? This includes our neighbors, our friends, our family, our coworkers, and so on. Since we regularly make time for entertainment, regular exercise, and hobbies, why can't we set aside a morning or an evening to talk with unbelievers about Jesus at a park, a local apartment complex, or at a university where students are looking to engage in conversations?

As Christians, we sometimes spend so much of our spare time with other believers that we become ineffective in having "Jesus Conversations" with unbelievers. The book of Acts tells us a story where Peter and John came across a beggar outside the temple where they were going to a prayer meeting. When he asked them for money, they could have said, "We're too busy to talk to you because we're headed to a prayer meeting that starts at three o'clock and we don't want to be late." Instead, Peter offered something greater. In the name of Jesus, Peter healed the man. When he jumped up and began praising God, a crowd began to surround them to see what had happened. Seeing this as an evangelistic opportunity, Peter addressed the crowd.

> "By faith in the name of Jesus, this man whom you see and know was made strong. It is Jesus' name and the faith that comes through him that has completely healed him, as you can all see. . . . Repent, then, and turn to God, so that your sins may be wiped out, that times of refreshing may come from the Lord, and that he may send the Messiah, who has been appointed for you—even Jesus." (Acts 3:16)

The Scriptures tell us that the church grew to about five thousand believers. In other words, up to two thousand were converted and became Christians in response to this miracle and Peter's bold proclamation of Jesus.

Excuse #9: "My Life Isn't What It's Supposed to Be"

No, maybe it's not. But if you have a relationship with Jesus, then you have something to share. You have a message of grace that God so loved the world—and you—that he sent Jesus, his only begotten

Son (John 3:16). Having a relationship with Jesus means that you can now follow after him and be a witness, like the apostles, to the inbreaking of the kingdom of God. Not only this, but you're going to spend eternity with him in heaven! Sure, you can be honest and share that your life is still a work in progress, but say that you're trusting in what Jesus has already done for you on the cross.

It also doesn't matter what sins you may have committed in the past. If you are forgiven in Christ's name, then you are forgiven. Instead of being used for "common purposes," God can cleanse you and use you now for "special purposes" (2 Tim. 2:20–21). Even King David was forgiven when he confessed to the serious sins of adultery and murder. After being confronted by Nathan the prophet, David cried out to God, saying,

> Create in me a pure heart, O God,
>   and renew a steadfast spirit within me.
> Do not cast me from your presence
>   or take your Holy Spirit from me.
> Restore to me the joy of your salvation
>   and grant me a willing spirit, to sustain me.
> Then I will teach transgressors your ways,
>   so that sinners will turn back to you.
>
> (Ps. 51:10–13)

After God cleansed and restored David, David wanted to teach other transgressors about the ways of the Lord. He didn't allow a grievous failure to silence him forever.

You may feel your spiritual life doesn't measure up. Maybe you're not a "100-watt light bulb," but even a little "7-watt bulb" (that is, a nightlight) shows up brightly in a dark room. So, let your light shine regardless! During his Sermon on the Mount, Jesus told the crowd, "You *are* the light of the world" (Matt. 5:16; my italics). He didn't say, "You need to try to improve your life, and maybe one day you'll become the light of the world." Right now, Jesus can shine through you when you're faithful and walking in obedience to him. In the book of Ecclesiastes, the "Teacher" says, "If you wait for perfect conditions, you will never get anything done. . . . Keep on sowing your seed, for you never know which will grow—perhaps it all will" (Eccl. 11:4–6 TLB). Yes, God can use *you!*

3

How Do You Start the Conversation?

How do we start a conversation about Jesus with a stranger? Or even with a close friend, coworker, or neighbor who is not a Christian? For a moment, let's think about the ordinary people we might encounter in our daily routines: the administrative assistant, our exercise partners, the commuter beside us on the Metro, the server at the restaurant, a hired vehicle driver, or our colleagues at work?

Isn't it true that we get so busy we don't see those around us or notice details that would help us start a conversation? Are we active or passive in initiating conversations and relationships? In the Great Commission, Jesus told us to "go into all the world," "preach the Gospel" (Mark 16:15), and "make disciples of all nations" (Matt. 28:19). He wants us to be active participants in this commission. It's nearly impossible to make disciples if people don't hear the good news and become believers. After all, they need to be believers before they can be discipled. But if we don't share the gospel with them, then how can they hear this news? We can't just passively wait for them to come to us. We need to overcome our fears and reach out to them.

The word *salt* is referenced multiple times in the Bible. Salt was used as a seasoning, a preservative, and a disinfectant. Jesus said, "You are the salt of the earth" (Matt. 5:13), and the apostle Paul wrote, "Let your conversation be always full of grace, seasoned with salt, so that you may know how to answer everyone" (Col. 4:6). Just as salt can bring out the best taste in food, so our speech should continually be gracious and bring forth goodness. In the ancient world, another purpose of salt was as a disinfectant to guard against contamination. Likewise, our speech should be grounded in truth and strong enough to discern error and falsehoods. Evangelist Rice Broocks shared with me the "S-A-L-T" acronym as a model for evangelism:

"S"   Start a Conversation

"A"   Ask Questions

"L"   Listen

"T"   Tell the Story (the gospel and your testimony)

In this chapter, we will focus on becoming people who start conversations. (In the next chapter, we will talk about asking unbelievers appropriate questions and becoming more effective listeners.)

In our daily lives, we must be willing to initiate dialogue with others. It's possible that we'll be rejected or that the other person simply won't want to talk about this. Other times, however, people *will* engage with us. So, how can you and I become intentional in starting conversations with those around us?

At this point, I'm not only talking about spiritual conversations but also about being friendly and just engaging in conversation. We need to be friendly and take a genuine interest in the other person. As Paul wrote, "Live wisely among those who are not believers and make the most of every opportunity" (Col. 4:5 NLT). You and I are not perfect, so there's no perfect way to start a conversation. But you can smile and speak up to someone. Following are some helpful suggestions.

Ways to Start a Conversation

Say "Hello"

Although *hello* is a simple word, how many of us have missed out on getting to know someone because we didn't say hello? How many love stories or songs have been inspired by a simple hello? In a helpful article, writer Gloria Furman said,

In whatever language you speak, your *hello* could initiate the first conversation among many that God uses to draw someone to himself. Maybe the first conversation becomes *the* conversation. "Hello" is a small word, but it says to someone, "I see you." And that means something to everyone, no matter where they're from in the world."[1]

Become a Great Noticer

Are you a great noticer? When you walk into a room, do you make an effort to notice people and details in that environment? When you encounter someone new, here's a suggestion: put down your phone (or whatever else is distracting you) and *really* look at that person. What is it about them that stands out to you? Their clothing? A tattoo? Their pet? Their beard? Their baby? Intentionally observe *something*. Is that a new flavor of coffee? What is the meaning of your wrist tattoo? Is it okay if I pet your dog? Reject passivity, pay attention to those around you, and courageously initiate a conversation—even if it's just about the weather.

Remember the Person's Name

We need to take genuine interest in people. Nobody wants to feel like a project. One of the best ways we can show people we love them is to remember their name and use it often while we're talking with them. In the Virginia community church I grew up in, there was an elderly lady named Christine "Mama" Knopp who had memorized thousands of people's names. Whenever there was a visitor at church, she made a point of getting to know them, even writing their name down in a guestbook.

Many of us claim to be "bad at names." But maybe the problem is that we don't really care for people the way Christ cares for them. It takes some effort to learn names and then remember them. I'm still working on getting better myself! It's embarrassing when I've met a medical assistant or receptionist several times and still don't remember what to call them.

It's an art to memorize people's names, so using the acronym "A-R-T," here are some tips that might help you:

1. "A" *Associate* the person with something that helps you remember them. For example, you might remember six-foot seven-inch Dave is from Dallas, so you remember, "Big Dave from Dallas," or Maria who works as a medical assistant as "Medical Assistant Maria."

2. "R" *Repeat* a person's name a few times when you first meet them. For example, I might say, "Maria, is your patient being compliant with his CPAP machine?" You may even ask the person how they spell the name and then spell it back to them. This repetition will help you remember.

3. "T" *Take* some notes on your phone or a notepad. After I talk to a person, I might take notes on my phone. Sometimes, I have a list of people I pray for, and I later transfer those names from my phone to my prayer journal. When I joined a new workout facility, I jotted down the names of several people. I know there is Sarah (super strong) and Cale (such a fast runner, he probably lives off kale).

If you struggle with names, work hard to learn the A-R-T of name memory, associating the person's name with something that helps you remember. You can repeat their name several times in the conversation, repeat the spelling if it's a difficult name, and later take notes in your phone or notepad that you can then add to your prayer journal. Here are some ideas of how to connect with those do not believe the way you do.

Invite People to Your Home for a Snack or a Meal

Have a "Matthew Party"! We read in Matthew 9:10 that "while Jesus was having dinner at Matthew's house, many tax collectors and 'sinners' came and ate with him and his disciples."

Recently, I invited several workout partners from the gym over to my house. There was a combination of both Christians and non-Christians, and some good spiritual conversations followed. While no one was converted, Jesus certainly came up in the conversation.

Every Thursday night, my parents (who are in their sixties) invite certain neighbors to play shuffleboard and games in their house. This had led to meaningful friendships and gospel-centered conversations. My father was even asked to speak at the funeral when one of the neighbors passed away.

I've been hosting a "seekers-of-truth" gathering in my house. A Hindu friend, who moved to Dallas from India, joined and asked many questions. He has not yet converted to Christianity, but after our initial meeting he sent me a message: "Thanks for inviting me. It is really great to learn about Jesus. I hope I didn't offend anyone." I assured him he didn't offend anyone by asking his questions. In this gathering, we have people from a variety of backgrounds. One of the guys seems to be influenced by Jehovah's Witness theology. We had four atheists join us last Sunday, and one of them agreed to meet with me for further conversation yesterday.

You too can host a seeker-friendly informal Bible study gathering in your own home for both believers and seekers. Here's our simple format. We eat and hang out from 6:00 to 6:30. I grill chicken and burgers for them, making sure to include a variety of veggies for my vegan friends. After dinner, I show about ten minutes of *The Gospel of John*, which is a "word-for-word film adaptation" (using the NIV translation) with Aramaic-speaking actors recreating the stories in the Fourth Gospel.[2] We watch one chapter per week and then discuss it for about thirty minutes. After that, I open up our time for questions about anything. I say that no question is off limits. We do this for an additional thirty minutes. Our whole gathering is less than two hours.

Last Sunday some of the questions included, "What about those who have never heard the gospel? Are they going to hell?" A couple of my Christian friends told me they feel much more comfortable inviting their unbelieving friends to my house than to church. I think having these conversations at home and sharing a meal may allow us to delve into deep questions that are not always easy at some churches.

Coach a Sports Team

This is a great way to connect with your child, their friends, and parents. When I was young, my father coached my little league basketball team and was able to be a witness. Later in life, I received permission through my home church to open our brand-new church gym to invite some of the best players in the community to play in a midweek pickup game. At half-time, I shared a short devotional that provided good reasons to trust in Jesus. Several of the players prayed to receive Christ and other players agreed to meet me on another day to read the Bible.

Host a "Jesus Conversations" Day

One Saturday morning a month, I invite my Christian friends to go with me to our local parks and share the gospel. We meet at my house or at a friend's home, where we have a simple breakfast at about nine o'clock. While we eat our breakfast, those who are gifted in evangelism share a few pointers about evangelism. After that, we do some role-playing and say a short prayer. An hour later, we split up into groups of two or three (so it's not obvious we're evangelizing) and then go out to start conversations at the local parks (if it's raining, we go to the local mall).

This method has been effective, and a number of people have given their life to Christ. Whenever someone is interested, I encourage my Christian friends to ask for their phone number and then follow up with them. I think it's important for us to talk intentionally to strangers about Jesus. Although many people find this method intimating, Jesus intentionally sent out his disciples to have conversations with strangers, and Paul and the other apostles intentionally started conversations with strangers. From a pragmatic standpoint, cults like Mormonism and Jehovah's Witnesses have grown through intentional door-to-door evangelism.

On one Saturday morning, my friend Justin Bass shared with our Jesus Conversations group some tips about evangelism. He told us his story of when he was a business major at Southern Methodist University. He and his girlfriend Allison were waiting in line to go into a crowded sorority Halloween party, both dressed up like devils. As they waited in line, they saw a young man sharing the gospel to the people ahead of them. As the young street evangelist boldly proclaimed Jesus and repentance, Justin became convicted of his sins even though he had no direct conversation. Late that night, Justin still couldn't help thinking about the young man's words about Jesus, so he searched for a Bible in his dorm. After reading the Gospels, Justin soon placed his trust in Jesus and started attending a church where he could learn the Bible.

Justin came to love Jesus so much that he enrolled at Dallas Theological Seminary where he earned a master's degree and then a doctoral degree in theology. He also married that girl who dressed like a devil with him. A couple years ago, Justin and Allison, along with their two children, moved to Amman, Jordan, to train pastors to proclaim the hope of the gospel. They now reach many people, but their lives were dramatically changed because of one ordinary young man took the risk to boldly talk to strangers about Jesus.

Do Evangelism at Your Local College and Community College

We don't have to travel the world to become missionaries: the world is coming to America. We can be missionaries in our own communities! Every year, there are hundreds of thousands of international students studying at American universities, many of whom will return to their native countries as leaders and influential persons.[3] Even during the COVID pandemic of 2020, I was enrolled in an online course at Harvard in biotechnology development, where I interacted with students living in other countries.

A couple years ago, I asked my friends at church to join me in evangelism outreach at the University of Texas at Dallas. I asked my friends to meet me at the food court on campus on Thursday evenings, where we shared the gospel to many students from India, China, and Pakistan who are Muslims, Hindus, and atheists. Pretty soon, we had about twenty Christians engaging in spiritual conversations and we saw a number of students give their lives to Christ.

We also partnered with a couple of ministries on campus for further conversation and follow up. One of the ministries was Reasonable Faith, where my friend Allen would invite a number of Christian apologists, scientists, and professors to give lectures on the historicity of Christianity. We also partnered with the Baptist Student Union, which hosted a free lunch, where we could invite students to consider the facts about Christ. What about you? Have you considered partnering with a local college ministry to serve international students who have moved to the United States?

Use the Arts and Music as a Tool for Evangelism

When we were sharing the gospel on a Saturday at Klyde Warren Park in Dallas, my friend Madison, who is a middle school art teacher, wanted to walk around the Dallas Museum of Art. She thought she could use her passion for art to initiate conversations with strangers that might lead to a spiritual conversation. At that time, the museum happened to be featuring the Keir Collection of Islamic Art. Madison noticed a young woman wearing a hijab admiring a Qur'an. Madison said hello to the young woman and they began a conversation that lasted for over an hour. After that, they exchanged phone numbers. Then Madison noticed another woman who was sitting alone and who seemed sad. She soon discovered the woman was being forced to marry someone she didn't want to marry. She was a Muslim and arranged marriages were practiced in her culture. Madison developed a friendship, got her phone number, and later met both ladies for lunch to tell them about Jesus.

On another occasion, with my friends Frank and Nathan, I co-hosted an art outreach called "The Easel" in Uptown Dallas. Some of the artists sang, one girl talked about her paintings, and someone stood up and rapped, while another did stand-up comedy. Through our outreach, a Muslim man in his twenties came to faith in Jesus after I presented the gospel to him.

Allow Your Job to Open Doors

In any line of work, we always have the opportunity to build relationships with others. I work full time in medical sales and frequently have opportunities to share the gospel. In medical sales, I am often asked questions about my previous career, when I worked with I Am Second, an evangelism ministry. One of my cardiologists was an avid LSU football fan, and I was able to tell him about doing an outreach with several of the LSU football players. Later, I gave a him a copy of my book *I Am Second* that tells stories of radical life changes.

When doctors ask me about books I have written, I go out to my car and grab one that I've written about Jesus and the truthfulness of Christianity. On one occasion, I had an extended conversation with a Jewish doctor, who is one of my best providers. We started by talking about his patients' sleep disorders and diabetes; but after closing my sales presentation, I was able to talk to him about my recent trip to Israel where I visited the Western Wall (also known as the Wailing Wall) and the Sea of Galilee. After I did a thorough job for my employer talking about obstructive sleep apnea, I guided the conversation toward Jesus. All these conversations provide me with an opportunity to build trust and a deeper relationship with my clients.

"Servant Evangelism" Often Opens Doors

Sometimes doing something for someone can open the door for a meaningful conversation. Growing up, I remember my dad would ask me to help the elderly neighbors shovel a driveway, clean out a gutter, or take care of their pets. Through this neighborly help over the years, my father has led various neighbors to Christ. Some people call this "servant evangelism," which is based on the idea that "God's kindness leads you toward repentance" (Rom. 2:4).

Be Truthful, but Don't be Manipulative or Condescending

To build relationships with unbelievers, we need to be willing to start conversations. We need to be bold in sharing the gospel, which means we shouldn't shy away from potentially confrontational words such as *sin* and *hell*. The gospel is not a manipulative sales pitch, nor is it something we should try to sugarcoat, leaving out the unpleasant call to repent of sin.

I know that salespeople get a bad rap (I'm one of them!), but I believe the best salespeople can be persuasive and also live a life of integrity. A lot of people say, evangelism shouldn't be a sales pitch. On one hand I agree, but on another hand I don't. It depends on how "sales pitch" is defined.

Someone may say, "A sales pitch is when one tries to persuade another person into buying something." I might respond, "That's a good definition! I like the way you said that so persuasively! You've changed my mind!" If that response goes over their head, I might ask, "Is it possible to use words to persuade someone to embrace an idea or product that is actually good?"

I think there is a way to speak persuasively with integrity. At work, I want to be an employee who is honest, asks good questions, and finds reasonable solutions. A Hindu friend once told me that he appreciated the honesty of the Christians he had met in business. King Solomon wrote, "The seeds of good deeds become a tree of life; a wise person wins friends" (Prov. 11:30 NLT).

Another important facet of successful sales that applies to evangelism is to avoid exaggerating or being manipulative when we talk about the gospel of Jesus. The apostle Paul said, "We reject all shameful deeds and underhanded methods. We don't try to trick anyone or distort the word of God. We tell the truth before God, and all who are honest know this" (2 Cor. 4:2 NLT). Some Christians, for example, talk only about promises of the great life the person will have after trusting in Jesus. For many of us, however, we know that more pain may enter a person's life after trusting in Jesus!

We must also be humble when we share God's truth with others. We don't want to come across as arrogant, know-it-all, or condescending. Paul writes, "For who makes you different from anyone else? What do you have that you did not receive?" (1 Cor. 4:7). We Christians are recipients of the grace of God. Without the grace of God, we would be as lost as the sinner we are talking to. Sometimes Christians have a reputation for being negative or antagonistic. We must be careful here. We want to be truthful, but we also must be gracious.

We Should Always Pray

Sometimes we may feel like we're not getting anywhere in the conversation. In his letters to the Corinthians, Paul says,

The man without the Spirit does not accept the things that come from the Spirit of God, for they are foolishness to him, and he cannot understand them, because they are spiritually discerned. (1 Cor. 2:14)

The god of this age has blinded the minds of unbelievers, so that they cannot see the light of the gospel of the glory of Christ, who is the image of God. (2 Cor. 4:4)

When we speak the gospel to unbelievers, we need to remember that apart from Christ we can do nothing (John 15:5). If someone shows no interest, we need to know when to stop. There have been times when I asked a person if they had any spiritual interests, but I could sense they had little interest in talking.

Sometimes after asking multiple questions about the faith, we need to have the wisdom to know when to stop. I think this is especially true with close family members and coworkers. We should pray for them and ask the Lord to give us wisdom to know how to initiate matters of faith. I tried to share the gospel with a friend and he immediately shut me down; but later, when his sister died of cancer, he seemed more open to talking about God.

It's also important to keep the long view in mind as you pray. My grandmother prayed for her four sons for twenty years without seeing any spiritual interest. Then, one year before she died, three of my uncles surrendered their lives to Christ!

I encourage you to create "top ten" prayer lists of people you pray for every day for their salvation. Every morning, review this list and pray for them, mentioning their names to God. When it feels like you're not getting anywhere, don't give up! Paul said, "Devote yourselves to prayer, being watchful and thankful" (Col. 4:2). When we pray, we not only want to mention their names, but we also need to pray persistently. I've had several people on my prayer list, and after a year of praying for them, one of them told me they wanted to join my Sunday night Bible study for seekers.

As Paul wrote, "Pray for us, too, that God may open a door for our message, so that we may proclaim the mystery of Christ, for which I am in chains" (Col. 4:3). Paul then asks the Colossians to pray that he would be able to explain the gospel with clarity: "Pray that I may proclaim it clearly, as I should" (Col. 4:4). We too need to pray for wisdom and clarity in our conversations of the gospel, but then we also act.

As we're praying, we also need to be careful in the way we interact with unbelievers. Paul said, "Be wise in the way you act toward outsiders; make the most of every opportunity" (Col. 4:5). What opportunities do you have to talk about Jesus to an unbeliever?

Pray that God will open the door and that when you speak you will clearly present the good news of the gospel. Then make the most of the opportunities you have—especially right now!

Our Love Will Impact People for Jesus

Jesus said, "Your love for one another will prove to the world that you are my disciples" (John 13:35 NLT). In his book *Organic Outreach for Ordinary People*, Kevin Harney writes,

> The starting point of effective outreach is not a system, a program, or a special presentation. It is a heart deeply in love with God and with people. Without love, no effective strategy will work. With God's love, we can change the world.[4]

It's not just our love for lost people that will get their attention, but also our love for other believers.

What do outsiders see when they visit our Christian groups or our churches? Do we show love to our fellow believers? Sometimes, it's our Christian friends we have difficulty loving consistently. What do we do when they gossip about us? Or hurt us? How quickly do we forgive them? How do we devote ourselves to them regularly? How do we serve them—in love—more effectively? If you're single, do you have roommates you can serve? How can you honor your family members and bless them? You see, it's when we love other Christians that non-Christians observe the way we act differently and take notice.

The apostle Peter encouraged first-century believers, "Above all, let your love for one another be intense, because love covers a multitude of sins" (1 Pet. 4:8). In the first three centuries, Christianity grew because of the way Christians loved one another. The early church fathers were committed to apologetics in persuading unbelievers about Christianity, but they were also committed to loving people even if they received no love in return. Tertullian, a second-century Christian leader, wrote how pagans were amazed by the witness of Christian love. "See how they love one another!" they would remark. A Greek document called the *Epistle of Mathetes to Diognetus* (AD 130) says about Christians, "They obey the prescribed laws, and at the same time, they surpass the laws by their lives. They love all men but are persecuted by all."

One way we can show practical love is by helping new converts leave an immoral profession or a living situation that isn't honoring to God. We can wisely help new believers financially until they find other employment. We can help them with their résumés, online professional profiles, and interviewing. My friend Lisa has a ministry that builds relationships with women who had jobs in strip clubs and prostitution and helps them get a new start through practical means.

I mentioned earlier that I volunteered for 40 Days for Life, a ministry that prays for women seeking to terminate their pregnancy. Founder Shawn Carney and his wife Marilisa prayed outside of Planned Parenthood in Bryan, Texas, for eight years. During this time, they built a relationship with the manager, Abby Johnson, by talking with her on the other side of a fence, showed her the love of Christ even though they were strongly opposed to Planned Parenthood murdering unborn children. They offered to help her find another job if she quit working for that organization.

Then one day, when a visiting abortionist asked Abby for assistance in the operating room, Abby watched the baby inside the womb move away from the instruments, fighting for her life. Abby was so shaken that she quit her job and talked to Shawn at The Coalition for Life. Shawn and Marilisa encouraged Abby and helped her in the process. Today, Abby works full time in this pro-life ministry, helping other workers in the abortion industry quit their jobs and transition into new life-affirming careers. Abby's story is told in the 2019 film, *Unplanned*.[5]

We have discussed several important facets in having meaningful conversations about Jesus—but remember, above all, it's our love for unbelievers that will win them over. Paul encourages us with these words:

> But above all these things put on love, which is the bond of perfection. (Col. 3:14 NKJV)

Some of you reading this book can probably remember a time when you were not walking with Christ. Do you remember a time when someone—especially a Christian—showed love to you? Did their actions of love inspire you to walk closer to Jesus? Likewise, if we truly love others, the Lord will open doors for us to have meaningful conversations.

4

ASKING BETTER QUESTIONS AND LISTENING

As we see in the Gospels, Jesus could talk with anyone. He could connect with children and tell stories everyone could understand, yet he could also effectively argue with the religious scholars and educated lawyers of his day. He initiated a conversation with a Samaritan woman who most Jews would shun; not only was she a woman, but she was also of a race they did not associate with. Ultimately, he stepped into the lives of some fishermen, telling them to throw out their nets, and then to follow him.

After starting a conversation, Jesus knew exactly what questions to ask. Throughout the Gospels, Jesus is recorded as asking 339 questions, all of them intentional and purposeful. As he is our model in so many ways, so Jesus is also our model conversationalist.

Jesus not only asked questions himself, but he also encourages us to ask questions. Jesus said, "Ask and it will be given to you. . . . For everyone who asks receives" (Matt. 7:7–8). In the previous chapter, we looked at ways to start conversations and build relationships with unbelievers. Now we want to look at how we can ask better questions and listen effectively.

In an excellent article titled "The Surprising Power of Questions," Harvard Business School professors Alison Wood Brooks and Leslie K. John wrote, "Few executives think of questioning as a skill that can be honed—or consider how their own answers to questions could make conversations more productive. That's a missed opportunity."[1]

It's also a missed opportunity when Christians don't hone their conversational skills by asking better questions to unbelievers. While it's true we want to love people, proclaim the simplicity of the gospel, and depend on the Holy Spirit, we shouldn't use these reasons as excuses to be bad stewards of the communication gifts God has given us. Jesus said, "For the people of this world are more shrewd in dealing with their own kind than are the people of the light" (Luke 16:8).

In this chapter, therefore, we want to look at how Jesus modeled the art of questioning. We can also learn from leaders in business, ministry, and psychology. In their article, Brooks and John say,

> "Be a good listener," Dale Carnegie advised in his 1936 classic *How to Win Friends and Influence People*. "Ask questions the other person will enjoy answering." More than 80 years later, most people still fail to heed Carnegie's sage advice. When one of us (Alison) began studying conversations at Harvard Business School several years ago, she quickly arrived at a foundational insight: People don't ask enough questions. In fact, among the most common complaints people make after having a conversation, such as an interview, a first date, or a work meeting, is "I wish [s/he] had asked me more questions" and "I can't believe [s/he] didn't ask me any questions."[2]

When we interview for a job or are in an important business meeting, we tend to try and sell ourselves by talking about ourselves.

The same is true with my Christian friends who get excited about apologetics. For many of us, apologetics played a significant role in either our conversion or spiritual growth. We drew closer to Jesus because we were convinced the Christian faith was *true*. But the craft of becoming a conversational apologist means listening and knowing *how* to ask good questions. In my youthful zeal, I often made the mistake of thinking that if I spewed out lists of facts to my unbelieving friends, this would persuade them to come to Jesus. Perhaps the problem isn't with the apologetics, but rather the overtalkative young apologist who doesn't listen.

Think about the last time you were in a job interview. Did you talk the whole time? Didn't you hold back once in a while? After all, aren't there some questions you should hold back on answering, such as your salary in your last job? Didn't you follow up with clarifying questions about the job? Isn't it important that we're able to ask specific questions to discern for ourselves if the job is a right fit for us?

If you're single and dating, do you try to sell yourself, or do you ask questions that allow your date to feel comfortable in discussing what *they* are passionate about? Do you use a variety of questions and tone? If we're comfortable with ourselves and can be pleasant with others, then we can ask the right questions and interject appropriate humor without coming across as obsessive or self-centered.

In dating, relationships, parenting, teaching, or business, if someone asks you a question you don't feel comfortable answering, are you discerning enough not to answer it? Perhaps your new date asks personal questions that would cause you to say something negative about the person you previously dated. You don't have to go there. The same goes with evangelism. Perhaps the person you're explaining the gospel to is trying to avoid any topic concerning Jesus. Maybe they want to take the conversation down a rabbit trail about secondary issues of religion and politics. You don't have to let them. But how can you wisely navigate the conversation? How can you exhibit your creativity?

Jesus' Model of Questioning

Let's first look at Jesus' model. On one occasion, when the political leaders were trying to trap him, he didn't immediately answer their question about whether it was right to pay taxes to Caesar or not. Rather, he said, "Show me a Roman coin. Whose picture and title are stamped on it?" (Luke 20:24 NLT). Notice his creativity.

Being the great noticer, Jesus made an observation about his surroundings. He asked for a coin, and then asked another question. People were drawn toward Jesus' ability to ask the real question—the question at the heart of the matter. Through his questions he helped people discover their own sincerity and their own beliefs.

Here is an example from the Gospel of John:

> By the Sheep Gate in Jerusalem there is a pool, called Bethesda in Hebrew, which has five colonnades. Within these lay a large number of the sick—blind, lame, and paralyzed [—waiting for the moving of the water, because an angel would go down into the pool from time to time and stir up the water. Then the first one who got in after the water was stirred up recovered from whatever ailment he had].
>
> One man was there who had been sick for 38 years. When Jesus saw him lying there and knew he had already been there a long time, He said to him, "Do you want to get well?" (John 5:2–6 HCSB)

Why did Jesus ask this? Isn't it insulting to ask a man suffering from paraplegia if he wants to be healed? In this case, however, it seems it wasn't just a matter of the man being able to walk again, but rather if he really wanted to be made well both physically and spiritually. We can only wonder since Jesus finds him later and tells him to stop sinning or something worse may happen to him (John 5:14).

The questions Jesus asked forced people to consider some deeper spiritual issues: in particular, who he really was and whether or not they believed in him. One of the best examples of this is when Jesus did not immediately answer a religious leader's political question but countered with a question.

> They arrived again in Jerusalem, and while Jesus was walking in the temple courts, the chief priests, the teachers of the law and the elders came to him. "By what authority are you doing these things?" they asked. "And who gave you authority to do this?"

Jesus replied, "I will ask you one question. Answer me, and I will tell you by what authority I am doing these things. John's baptism—was it from heaven, or of human origin? Tell me!"

They discussed it among themselves and said, "If we say, 'From heaven,' he will ask, 'Then why didn't you believe him?' But if we say, 'Of human origin' . . . " (They feared the people, for everyone held that John really was a prophet.)

So they answered Jesus, "We don't know."

Jesus said, "Neither will I tell you by what authority I am doing these things." (Mark 11:27–33)

Boom! Jesus, of course, is brilliant. He took control of the conversation with graciousness and confidence, but he didn't take the bait of his critics. Instead, with some careful questions, he gave them something to think about.

Three Benefits of Asking Questions

In life and in business, Professor Brooks says that one of the obvious benefits of asking questions is *information exchange*. "When I ask you questions . . . I'm going to learn what's in your mind."[3] So, if we're talking to someone of another faith, we need to find out what they think, what's in their mind. Jesus asked his disciples, "But what about you? Who do you say I am?" (Matt. 16:15). Even if a person is a Mormon, they may not hold to everything other Mormons believe. The first benefit of asking questions will allow you to discover how to share the gospel with this person.

A second benefit of asking questions in evangelism is an *increase in personal liking*. As Brooks explains, "When I ask questions, I show that I'm interested in learning and what's in your mind, I seem very responsive to you and empathic and I'm taking your perspective and I care about you." We don't want to be manipulative and ask questions just so people will like us. It's always helpful to follow Christ's "Golden Rule" of treating others as you would want to be treated. When we respect others, it's more likely they will respect us as well.

The third reason is *persuasion*. Rather than just preach to someone, we can ask questions and allow the person to discover the truth. This opens up the door for proclaiming the gospel. We'll come back to some persuasive techniques in questioning, but let's first consider the power of follow-up questions.

The Attractiveness of Follow-Up Questions

According to this study at Harvard Business School, the authors conclude that "not all questions are created equal." According to their survey, follow-up questions "seem to have a special power."

> They signal to your conversation partner that you are listening, care, and want to know more. People interacting with a partner who asks lots of follow-up questions tend to feel respected and heard. An unexpected benefit of follow-up questions is that they don't require much thought or preparation.[4]

In a conversation with someone you meet in Dallas, you might ask them if they were born in Texas. This then allows the person to give you more information about themselves: "No, I moved here three years ago from New York." At this point, you could ask something random. But it's much better to follow up with a related question: "I visited New York last month to see *Hamilton* on Broadway. In what part of New York did you live?" This is much more effective than asking random questions or switching the subject completely, which can seem more like an interview. When you ask a follow-up question specific to their answer (i.e., New York), you show that you have an interest in them being from New York.

Or you could ask specifically about *why* they moved here three years ago. Favor the follow up question. If you asking if they have any spiritual interests and they say, "I used to be Catholic." You may gently comment, "I'm not Catholic, but I'm curious. Why did you leave Catholicism?" All of these types of questions can help begin a beneficial conversation, and perhaps even give you a chance to share your Christian faith.

Ask "What" Questions

When asking questions, we can start by asking simple "what" questions. An easy "what" question that helps the conversation focus more on the other person is to ask, "What do you think about . . . ?" Before sharing your position on Jesus, the Bible, or a current political issue, try to get them talking. "What do you think about this new documentary on Jesus?" "What do you think about Jesus?" "What do you think about the church?" A second "what" question can bring more *clarification*. In an evangelistic conversation if someone says a theological word, ask them to clarify: "What do you mean by that?"

I was in a conversation with a young woman who was a conservative political leader. I wanted to discover if she was a Christian, so I asked her, "Are you a spiritual or religious person?" She responded, "I'm more spiritual." Although this is a popular term today, I didn't want to assume that she believed what another person means when they claim they're "more spiritual."

Wanting to follow up with a *clarifying* question, I asked, "What do you mean by *spiritual*?" Then I listened to her response. When she tried to define "spiritual," she revealed her lack of certainty of what she thought she believed. I listened to her, but it was important for me to ask further clarifying questions. Through our discussion, I learned that she had grown up as a Christian and considered herself to be a Christian but didn't believe in going to church. Asking clarifying questions like "What do you mean by . . ." or "Did you have a bad experience with church?" helped me discover her story and beliefs.

We want to be kind in starting a conversation and listening, but soon into the conversation, we may directly ask them one of these questions:

- Do you believe in God?

- Are you a religious or a spiritual person?

- Can I ask you some questions about what's happening in our world?

- Do you have a faith?

This past summer (2020), our country grieved the unjust death of George Floyd, and then for those who died in the protests and riots that followed.

During this time, my friend Brandon and I initiated a number of spiritual conversations as we walked around Dallas. Brandon suggested we start by talking about the nature of morality in light of current events. He was right, and we quickly found that people were willing to engage with us.

This is how we started the conversation: "Hi! Would it be okay if I asked you a question about some of the things happening in our world?" If the person said yes or asked us why, then we responded, "A lot of people are concerned about the injustices taking place in our world and I'm curious: Do you believe morality is objective (that is, knowable and true for all people, at all times, and all places), or do you think morality is subjective (that is, you have your morals, I have mine, and we shouldn't impose our morals on each other)? What are your thoughts? Their response not only allowed us to ask follow-up questions, but also to listen to their story and experience. We were then able to talk about the nature of sin, and the true remedy, which is the gospel of Christ.

Ask "Why" and "How" Questions

If someone says, "I don't believe morality is absolute. It's all relative and a construct of society," you could simply say, "Help me understand your position. Why do you believe that?" Or you could ask, "So, why do you think believe that a cop murdering an innocent human (without a trial) is just relatively wrong and not absolutely objectively wrong? Is that really just a relative opinion or is really objectively wrong?"

In evangelizing and appealing to morality, consider picking a current ethical issue on which they may likely agree with you. You may not need to prove objectivity immediately, but it's likely you'll hear some inconsistencies by just asking "why" questions. Let's suppose someone makes the statement: "Science disproves God." You could respond with a "why" question rather than jumping in with arguments for God's existence. Here are two questions you can ask to help you understand why they think the way they do:

- "Why do you believe that?"

- "Why are you so passionate about that?"

Here are some good questions for clarification:

- "How did you come to that conclusion?"

- "How do you know that to be true?"

- "Where did you get your information?"

- "Can you explain your statement to me?"

If someone says, "If God really existed, he would not allow suffering," rather than quote a Scripture immediately, ask them, "How do you know that to be true?" As Christians, it is important for us to give an answer; but if someone seems to be against our faith, we can calmly ask "why" or "how" questions and then listen while we look for an opportunity to share the truth.

About a year ago on a flight from Washington, DC, to Dallas, I was upgraded to first class. I sat beside a white woman, Anne, a social worker, advisor, and consultant who had served in politics for some time. We said hello, and she asked me what book I was reading. I responded by telling her that I was reading C. S. Lewis's *Screwtape Letters*. She told me she hadn't read the book but that she had an appreciation for him, and I said that I appreciated Lewis's insights into Christianity. Thinking my exchange with her had gone well, I picked up the book to continue reading, when she raised her voice and said, "You are the problem."

Naturally, I was taken aback.

"Well, maybe not you specifically," she said, "but white men." She then told me about the injustices perpetrated by white men and how we have oppressed women and the poor. She told me how it was so unfair that she gets less respect than her husband, even though she makes three times more money.

Although she had attacked me out of the blue, I decided to be gracious. I asked questions and listened to her for a while, and then I asked if she believed in God. She said everything is god, but she considered herself an agnostic. So I asked her, "Do you believe that human life is more exceptional and more valuable than other animal life?"

She said no.

I asked her if she was a vegetarian.

She said, "Most of the time. On rare occasions, I eat meat."

I smiled. "If animals are just as valuable as humans, then how do you justify eating other animals, even on rare occasions?"

"Well, my husband is vegan." She then shifted the conversation to some hot topics in politics and religion, including global warming and abortion. Eventually, I calmly shared the gospel and talked about Jesus and forgiveness.

She didn't believe the Gospels were reliable. She said we don't have anything written about Jesus until the third century.

I asked her, "Why did you believe that?"

She said, "I read about it in a magazine."

"How do you know that the journalist who wrote that article accurately described the historical narrative? After all, even agnostic scholars, like Bart Ehrman at the University of North Carolina Chapel Hill, affirm that we have multiple contemporary sources about Jesus from the first century."

Although she had no answer to that, she tried to affirm that Jesus had a lot of good things to say. I then told her how the first-century

Jesus was compassionate toward women in a way that was countercultural in that time period. I also talked about the case of the historical resurrection and how women were the first to discover the empty tomb. Toward the end of the conversation, she told me I had a lot of potential to be a voice for humanity and especially women. "There's something different about you," she said. She told me she didn't think I was like other white men she had either encountered or knew about. "You, as a man, can be a humanist for all people, for women, for equality. I see it in you. You're different from other Christians."

As you might guess, I didn't convert her, but here was a wealthy, influential woman in politics who wanted to attack me for being white, for being a man, for being a conservative, and for being a Christian. I asked questions and listened to her, but I also tried to help her discover the inconsistencies of some of her own way of thinking. Although we didn't end in mutual agreement on various issues, I certainly gave her some food for thought. I like what apologist Greg Koukl says,

> Remember, my goal is modest. I want to put a stone in the person's shoe. I want to get him thinking. I want him to consider listening to Jesus first before dismissing him. If I can simply open that door, I have accomplished something important.[5]

Isn't It Possible?

After you've talked with someone for a while, here's another great question to ask: "Isn't it possible . . . ?" With this question, you're not asking them if they *agree* with your position completely but just to admit that your position is *possible*. Suppose you're in a discussion about the existence of God with an agnostic. You might ask, "Isn't it possible that if there is a moral law, there needs to be a moral lawgiver?" Notice, I'm not asking them to believe in a Moral Lawgiver with absolute certainty; I'm just asking them to consider a moderate, open-minded agnostic approach.

Have You Considered?

Another similar question is to ask, "Have you considered . . . ?" For example: "Have you considered what the best explanation may be for the fine-tuning of the universe?" If you don't think someone is willing to listen to you, then you might ask, "Do you consider yourself an open-minded person?" If they consider themselves as "tolerant" or "progressive," then if you ask this question, you put them in a dilemma. If they say no, then they contradict their claim of being tolerant. But if they say, "Yes, I'm open-minded," then they don't have a reason to shut you up if you suggest a different way of thinking. This happened to me on a flight from Wisconsin to Texas.

After speaking at a fundraiser for Wisconsin Right to Life, I was packing for my flight back to Dallas when I sensed the Holy Spirit prompting me to carry along one of my Christian books in case I got into an interesting spiritual conversation. As I was waiting in the airport, I saw a tall, blond woman sitting nearby who seemed familiar. I soon realized it was Cecile Richards, CEO of Planned Parenthood at the time (2015). She had recently been on the news because of allegations that the organization had been adjusting their abortive procedures so they could sell body parts for profit.

As a pro-life activist, I wanted to talk with her, but I had no idea if she would even give me the time of day. I knew, however, that Christ wanted me to offer her the message of his mercy. Walking over to where she sat, I introduced myself and told her I was pro-life. I pulled out a copy of *We Choose Life*[6] and explained that it included stories of friends like Jewels and Ramona who had left the industry.

"Why do you call us an industry?" she asked.

"You perform 300,000 abortions every year."

"We provide safe healthcare for women."

I looked her in the eye and calmly said, "Cecile, you and I both know there is nothing safe about taking a sopher clamp in a DE and crushing down on—"

That's when she interrupted and things got awkward. Although she didn't want to continue the conversation, she said she'd take my business card. Before I walked away, I decided to ask her one more question: "Cecile, do you consider yourself an open-minded person?" (As I mentioned earlier, when a conversation becomes confrontational, this might be good to ask if they claim to value tolerance and a variety of ideas.)

She shot back in a stern voice, "I'm very open minded!"

I calmly responded, "Well, wonderful! Perhaps you will consider reading this book, even if you disagree with it. I've read material by leading defenders of abortion like Peter Singer; and even though I strongly disagree with him, it's helpful for me to understand his position." I handed her *We Choose Life* and then returned to my seat.

I have no idea what she did with the book. Part of me thinks she probably threw it in the trash can. What I do know is that Jesus has the power to save anyone who cries out to him. If Jesus can redeem Dr. Bernard Nathanson, the founder of NARAL (National Abortion and Reproductive Rights Action League), who did more abortions than anyone else in America at the time, then he can certainly touch the heart of someone like Cecile Richards.

Ask Hard, Direct Questions

Sometimes we have mixed goals in conversations. We want to have fun. We want to get to know someone. We want to increase our business. We also want to be a witness for Christ. In having spiritual conversations, I used to assume I should start with broad, open-ended questions rather than tough, closed-ended questions. There have been times when I felt afraid that my tough questions would be too direct, judgmental, or rude, and then I'd lose the opportunity to ever talk to that person again. It's natural for us to think that easing our way into the conversation is always better. But this is not always the case. Leslie K. John, in her research at Harvard, said that in some competitive business situations, "we actually found that people disclosed more . . . when you started with the most sensitive question."[7] Her previous perspective was that you warm up and start with easy questions and then gradually build rapport, but she discovered that the opposite can actually lead to more revelation.

I'm convinced that most of the time, people will appreciate our directness rather than vagueness or "beating-around-the-bush." In medical sales, for example, I used to think I needed to talk about sports or family before pitching about the service I was selling. But I came to realize that if I was direct with the physicians in why I was there and asked for the sale early in the conversation, then they were willing to open up and share about other aspects of their lives. A doctor seemed to trust me when I was direct and asked tough questions to start with. If I had asked other questions first, the doctor may have wondered, "What's his mixed motive? Is he genuinely interested in what I did this past weekend?" I think the same is true in evangelism. Sometimes you can have greater effectiveness of jumping in with the tough questions sooner in the conversation than later. A lot of people will respect your forthrightness.

When I'm taking a group of friends out to engage in conversations, sometimes I'm direct with people and say something like, "Hi! My name is Dave, and these are my friends. We're followers of Jesus, and we're out meeting new people and having conversations. Would it be okay if I asked you if you believe in God?" That's right to the point. I'm not holding brochures or signs, but they don't have to second-guess why I'm approaching them. If I'm on my own and want to strike up a conversation with someone, I try to find common ground first: I notice their dog or their tattoo or something else I can casually comment on. But if I'm taking a group out for the sole purpose of evangelizing, I frequently start with a clear introduction. After greeting them, I tell them my name and then ask a direct question. My tone is pleasant, and I normally smile, but they don't have to guess my motives.

Listen and Appeal to Logic

There are times when a conversation may become intense, and we feel an urgency to interrupt the other person to set something straight, but this isn't good—nor is it polite. Here are a couple of helpful Scripture passages to remember:

> He who answers before listening—that is his folly and his shame.
> (Prov. 18:13)

> Everyone should be quick to listen, slow to speak. (James 1:19)

Whenever we listen—really listen—we show people we care about them. When you're engaged in a spiritual conversation and sense the person is attacking your faith, there is a powerful tool on your side: Logic. During such an attack, a person may make a self-defeating statement; that is, a statement that fails to meet its own standard.

For example, if someone said "I can't speak a word of English" in English, this would be a self-defeating statement. Why? Because he or she just spoke that sentence in English! In the same way, if someone says, "There is no absolute truth!" you could respond with, "Is that absolutely true?" If so, then they have just contradicted themselves. If someone says, "You can't know any truth about God!" You can respond by asking, "How do you *know* that about God being unknowable?" If they still don't understand the significance of your question, you can ask, "When you say that we can't know any truth about God, isn't this a truth-claim you're professing to know?"

Actress and singer Mandy Moore was once asked, "What's your biggest pet peeve now that you've been in the industry a while?" She responded, "I don't like people who are intolerant—whether it be of race or religion or sexual preference. It really gets me going." If I had been there, I would have calmly asked her, "But aren't you being intolerant of intolerant people?"

Now, we have to be careful here because our goal is not just to win the argument or make the person look stupid. You want to help them discover their inconsistency. So, I suggest having *both clarity and charity*, while revealing any inconsistencies in the form of the question.

Genetic Fallacy

Another fallacy prevalent in our culture is the genetic fallacy, which is a fallacy of irrelevance. An example of the genetic fallacy would be if you provided evidence both philosophically and scientifically for the life of an unborn person, and someone shot back at you, "You as a man can't talk about abortion because you're a man and can't get pregnant!" This statement is a genetic fallacy, which implies that your statement is irrelevant solely based on someone's origin, gender, history, or source rather that the statement's truthfulness. Examples of this fallacy are:

- "You can't make moral judgments about a woman unless you're a woman!"

- "You shouldn't make ethical comments about race issues unless you're a minority!"

- "You can't talk about Islam unless you're a Muslim!"

- "You can't make judgments about same-sex marriage because you're straight!"

Any rational thinking will reveal the utter nonsense of such statements. Yet, I see Christians sometimes shy away from these types of intimidating conversation stoppers.

In reality, the truthfulness of your statement is true based on the *words* and *context* of the sentence, not because of your gender or tone. Truth-claims do not have gender. Truth does not have a tone. Statements are true or false regardless of who says them. A good definition of truth is "that which corresponds to reality." Simply put, truth is "telling it like it is." Something can be true even if the person saying it is of a different gender or origin.

So, don't ever allow these genetic fallacies to stop you from speaking the truth. Stand your ground! When people use the genetic fallacy on the issue of abortion and tell me my position is invalid because I'm a man, I respond, "If men's opinions on abortion are invalid simply because they are male, then wouldn't that invalidate the decision of *Roe v. Wade* since it was decided by seven out of nine men?" Or, "Isn't it true that approximately half of babies in the womb are male? What's your basis for making a moral judgment on their behalf?"

Ask the person using the genetic fallacy a question in return, and then confidently yet graciously guide the conversation to help them discover their fallacious inconsistencies. When you help someone believe in the nature of truth by asking the right questions, they might become more open to believing that Jesus is true. Truth is a cornerstone to having meaningful conversations. When we ask good questions and listen to people, we can help them take a step toward the truth.

In the apostle Paul's last letter, he concludes with excellent advice concerning our communicating with spiritually needy people (whom we mentioned in the last chapter). Consider the Amplified Bible's translation of this passage:

> Behave yourselves wisely [living prudently and with discretion] in your relations with those of the outside world (the non-Christians), making the very most of the time *and* seizing (buying up) the opportunity. Let your speech at all times be gracious (pleasant and winsome), seasoned [as it were] with salt, [so that you may never be at a loss] to know how you ought to answer anyone [who puts a question to you]. (Col. 4:5–6)

5

MEMORY TOOLS TO
EXPLAIN THE GOSPEL

I grew up going to church regularly, and I attended a Christian school where I was taught the gospel. But if you had asked me back then to define what we mean by "gospel," I might have faltered on some important aspects—like accidentally forgetting to mention the resurrection! Certainly, I would have part of the gospel correct, because I was taught the Bible and believed it was true; yet I didn't feel comfortable talking about it to my coworkers or friends who didn't believe the way I did.

In this chapter, we're going to look at ways to explain the gospel by using verses from memory and just *one Bible verse and a bridge analogy*. We'll also learn several diagnostic questions to ask a person to help them discover that they're a sinner and need to hear the good news of Jesus Christ.

As I mentioned earlier, God will frequently use a believer (or even a brand-new believer) to simply share what they know without using a lot of theological details. In the last chapter, we saw the Samaritan woman when she encountered Jesus for the first time: she hurried into her town and told everyone, "Come, see a man who told me everything I ever did. Could this be the Messiah?" (John 4:29). If you're a new believer, start with *what you know*. You will continue to learn as you engage in conversations about Jesus.

If you've been a Christian for some time and have been attending church, however, then this chapter is to encourage you to grow in your wisdom and skills in evangelism. Can you articulate the gospel with verses you know by heart? If not, hopefully by the end of this chapter, you'll have some tools to help clarify your communication of the good news to someone who doesn't believe the way you do!

Scripture Memory Prepares the Way

When I was in the eleventh grade, my mom asked me a question that would begin to change my life. She asked if I would like to become a decision counselor at Steve Wingfield's evangelistic outreach event. I did. So, I went through a series of trainings to learn how to explain the gospel to new converts.

Later, about a hundred churches came together for a large evangelistic crusade. When Steve gave the invitation, many people came forward publicly to make a decision to receive Christ. I would then meet with these new converts who were ready to either learn more about the gospel or place their faith in Jesus. During the training, I had to memorize a few verses and be able to articulate the simple doctrines of the gospel. Each evening as Steve gave a message from the Bible, I would scan the audience and pray. On a couple of occasions, I watched the person I was praying for get up and walk forward to make a decision to trust Christ.

Let's suppose you're in a conversation with your coworker, or a neighbor, or perhaps the person you see at the gym regularly. If you had three minutes to talk about the gospel, what would you say? What if you only had twenty seconds? We know that we could talk for hours explaining the details of Christ's salvation; but in this chapter, we're going to work on telling the gospel essentials in a way an unbeliever can easily and quickly understand.

Some people say, "Well, I just tell my story." Let me agree that your story is indeed important, but your story is not the gospel. Rather your story is *evidence* of the gospel changing your life. Relying on one's personal testimony or simply inviting someone to church may be missing out on actually speaking the gospel to them.

Though your personal experience is real and intriguing, the details in your conversion may not apply to other spiritual seekers from different life situations.

When I talk to Mormons or people from other cult groups and ask them, "Why are you a Mormon?" Most of them give me two reasons: (1) "I grew up a Mormon," or (2) "I've had this experience, and I've prayed about it." Just because they grew up in a faith and or had some "experience" or "feeling" does not mean it's necessarily true. I've heard Christians say the same thing! Some Christians get defensive when I push back, and they say, "You can't argue with someone's testimony." My response: "Isn't it true that lawyers argue with people's testimonies every day in the court of law?"

Don't get me wrong. I'm not against personal testimony. I just think we've relied on it too much in a way that is inconsistent with the New Testament and early church. I do, however, encourage you to write out your story and then practice saying it in four minutes in a way that's compelling and easy to understand for the non-Christian seeker—but always *including the good news of Christ.* Include God's story in your story. Let's make sure Jesus always gets the glory!

For these next two chapters, I must emphasize the most important story is the gospel, God's story. As we know, the gospel means "good news," and I want to share with you several methods that can help you organize your thoughts about the gospel that will enable you to easily explain it. Let me give you a reason why this is important. I once asked one of my pastor friends, who is one of the strongest Christians I know, "What are the main essentials of the gospel that are necessarily true and a person must believe in order to be saved?" He took a few minutes to tell me that God loved the world so much that Jesus died, and that the gospel is a gift and not achieved by works. I agreed, but after listening to him, I noticed he never mentioned that Jesus rose from the dead. When he finished, I asked him if there were any other details one must believe. He couldn't remember. Now, keep in mind, this is one of the most gifted evangelists I have met. This was simply a mindless mistake. Obviously, my friend believed that Jesus rose from the dead, but he forgot this essential fact when explaining the most important aspects of the gospel. Paul told the church at Corinth:

> For what I received I passed on to you *as of first importance*: that Christ died for our sins according to the Scriptures, that he was buried, *that he was raised on the third day* according to the Scriptures. . . . *If Christ has not been raised*, our preaching is useless and so is your faith!" (1 Cor. 15:3–4, 14; my italics)

Since the resurrection is continually mentioned in the New Testament, in this chapter we'll talk about what the gospel is along with some good verses and analogies to memorize. Yes, *memorize*!

Sometimes people will tell me, "Dave, I'm just not that good at memorizing Scripture like you." I used to say the same thing back when I attended my father's Christian high school in Staunton, Virginia. My father was my eleventh-grade Bible teacher, and I would say, "Dad, I just don't have that good of a memory. I can't memorize Bible verses." Now around this time, I had bought a couple guitars and was learning country songs by artists like Garth Brooks and George Strait. My dad smiled and said, "Dave, that's not true. You know all the words to hundreds of country songs! You have a very sharp memory. You can hear a country song a couple times and have all the lyrics memorized. You can do the same with Scripture." Looking back, I know my dad was right. Years later, after I became more serious about following Jesus, I memorized hundreds of verses. Don't underestimate your abilities!

Little did I know that several years later, I would be teaching Bible to twelfth-grade students at Prestonwood Christian Academy in Plano, Texas. Sometimes my students (who reminded me a lot of my former self) would tell me, "I'm not good at memorizing. I can't do this every week, Mr. Sterrett." Yet, a couple of these young men were extremely good at baseball and could tell me details about their favorite team and players. A couple of the others were gifted in drama and could memorize pages of dialogue for their performance. The truth is that we can memorize things we *love*. We memorize things we care about because they are important to us. As we continue loving Jesus with not only our heart but also our mind, we will love him by working hard to block out distractions to think about his word. On one hand, I want to emphasize that God can certainly use you while you don't have all the answers; yet on the other hand, it's important for you to grow in your knowledge. Even Jesus grew intellectually in his human nature: "And Jesus grew in wisdom and stature, and in favor with God and man" (Luke 2:52). We are also told to "grow in the grace and knowledge of our Lord and Savior Jesus Christ" (2 Pet. 3:18).

When we start a new job, we usually have to go through some training—some of which isn't very exciting! But that training usually gets us off on the right start with the company. If you're like me, you learned a lot in the training, but you also learned more as you went. It was that initial set of training, however, that provided a foundation of core knowledge.

Three years ago, when I was training for my current full-time job in medical sales, I crammed pages of memorization all about the severe health risks of obstructive sleep apnea, such as hypertension, diabetes, and heart failure, and I learned about symptoms such as snoring, daytime drowsiness, and high blood pressure. I sat under the teaching of multiple sales experts, as well as Dr. Michael Coppola, a nationally recognized sleep expert who has trained other sleep doctors and written numerous peer-reviewed articles. Within days of training at our headquarters in Glen Burnie, Maryland, I had memorized pages of details about a device that can test a patient in the comfort of their own home while wirelessly transmitting the data to Dr. Coppola and his team of pulmonologists to interpret the test results. Several executives in the company grilled me with questions during the training, to which I had to respond with poise. Not only did I memorize pages in a training book, but I also practiced good questions to ask physicians. After the training, I wrote down some of the sales training on three-by-five notebook cards. I learned from the top sales leaders in my company and wrote down the best questions to ask physicians.

How does all that apply to evangelism? In a similar way to our work-related training, it's good for us to be trained in spiritual disciplines like evangelism. What if you took a day or even a half day to be alone with God and fast, pray, and memorize Scripture? I've done this recently, and the Holy Spirit gave me a renewal and passion for evangelism.

Here's another Scripture memorization tip to consider. Before you go to bed, leave your phone in a different room and leave your computer and television off. Studies show that looking at your screen before you go to bed can disrupt your sleep. Instead, take a three-by-five card and write down a Bible verse. Write out the reference and the verse, and then write the reference a second time after the verse. At the top of your card, write out the topic. Remember to leave your phone in another room. For me, I purchased an old alarm clock. Before I go to sleep, I read a verse and reference out loud. When I awake, I again read that verse out loud. Throughout the day, I keep my notecards with me or in my car. This helps me from getting too easily distracted on my phones by mindless things on social media or sports. When I have some spare moments, I get my cards out and review the Bible verse.

I sometimes use Bible apps, but I prefer simple note cards to help me avoid distractions from alerts on my phone. These verses will not only help you become a more effective evangelist but will help draw you closer to the Lord as you think about them and pray over them. They will also help you live the gospel in a way that pleases the Lord and makes you a more effective witness. Psalm 119:11 says, "I have hidden your word in my heart that I might not sin against you." First Peter 2:2 says, "Like newborn babies, crave pure spiritual milk, so that by it you may grow up in your salvation." Just as we need food, we need spiritual milk if we are going to grow in evangelism.

In my business, doctors are busy and I usually have only a few seconds to talk to them and stir their curiosity about our company's service. Other times, I can dialogue for three or four minutes. When that happens, I take initiative to schedule a luncheon with the office. On those occasions, physicians will actually sit down and have lunch with me where I have an in-depth conversation for thirty minutes. When I'm having a lunch, it's real dialogue. Based on discernment and the personality of the doctor, I may jump right into the conversation of why I am there; while other times, I'll ask some questions to learn more about the doctor, how their day is going or perhaps a little about their vacation. I'm not doing this just so I can make a sale. As a representative of my company, I take a genuine interest in the person I am meeting. Even though I don't use all the material I used in my medical sales training, it was extremely important for me to memorize all those facts. I may not use all the material, but I'm prepared. And it's a process. I continue learning and reading peer-reviewed articles and listening to audio business books as I drive. I think it's similar to growing in personal evangelism. Since you're reading this book, I'm guessing you're interested in improving your evangelistic skills!

The apostle Paul emphasized to Timothy, his younger worker, the importance of being trained in sound biblical doctrine.

> Be a good servant of Christ Jesus, being *trained* in the words of the faith and of the good doctrine that you have followed . . . *train yourself* for godliness, while bodily training is of some value, godliness is of value in every way, as it holds promise for the present life and also for the life to come. (1 Tim. 4:6–7 ESV; my italics)

What is the first thing you do in the morning? Some people train their body with a workout. What about training your soul first by memorizing God's word and then working out? It may mean you need to discipline yourself to get to bed earlier. That's certainly been true in my life! If we train ourselves in our jobs and exercise, then we also should apply ourselves to growing in knowing the gospel and learning ways to become better communicators of it. When you're having a spiritual conversation, you may not have to share everything you know, but it's good to grow by memorizing Scripture and learning how to ask better questions (which we will discuss in future chapters).

The "Romans Road"

Where should you start with explaining the gospel? My first suggestion is to start by memorizing the four passages of what's commonly called the "Romans Road." This "road" is a simple and powerful way of explaining the good news of Jesus by citing only a few verses from Paul's letter to the church in Rome. I encourage you to get an old-school spiral notebook and write down the following verses—in this order—and memorize them word for word.

For all have sinned and fall short of the glory of God. (Rom. 3:23)

This verse emphasizes that every single person has sinned against God. Sin is disobedience and rebellion against God. We have disobeyed God, not only in our actions but also in our thoughts and evil desires. This leads to the next verse, which describes the penalty of sin.

For the wages of sin is death, but the gift of God is eternal life in Christ Jesus our Lord. (Rom 6:23)

The penalty of sin is death. Not just physical death but spiritual death, eternally separated from God. "It is appointed for man to die once, and after that comes the judgment" (Heb. 9:27). There are two destinations: heaven and hell. Although this may seem hopeless, we have good news in the next verse.

***But God demonstrates his own love for us in this: While we were
still sinners, Christ died for us. (Rom. 5:8)***

Think about this: at the time when you were the most sinful, selfish,
lustful, lazy, blasphemous, hateful, Jesus loved you. He loved you so
much, he died for you and took your punishment on the cross. This
leads us now to ask, how do we receive eternal life?

***If you declare with your mouth, "Jesus is Lord," and believe
in your heart that God raised him from the dead, you will be
saved. For it is with your heart that you believe and are justified,
and it is with your mouth that you profess your faith and are
saved. (Rom. 10:9–10)***

Notice the truths that are all affirmed in this one passage: Jesus is
Lord, Jesus died, Jesus rose again from the dead. This verse also says
that if you believe this gospel in your heart, then you are justified before God. "Justification" is a legal transaction in which God removes
the penalty of your guilt. God is not only perfectly loving, but he is
also holy and just. His perfect justice demands a perfect payment. But
only God is perfect, so God the Son, the Second Person of the Trinity,
took to himself a human nature in the incarnation. This incarnate
Son of God is Jesus, who took your sin on himself on the cross as a
substitution for you. Then Jesus clothed you with his perfect righ-
teousness. So, justification is "just-as-if-I'd never sinned." But it's more
than that: justification before God's eyes is just as if I'd always done
everything right and been perfect like Jesus. Incredible! The good
news is that anyone can receive this salvation by believing in their
heart and confessing that "Jesus is Lord." Salvation is not complicated!

Although these four verses of the "Romans Road" can be easily
explained in order, you may adapt. Memorize these verses so you
have the reference and verse down perfectly. Start with one or two
verses a week until you know them all. Remember, though, that when
you're having a conversation with someone, you don't necessarily

have to quote every single word (and certainly not the references), but it is good to be prepared so you know where the verse is located.

"One-Verse Evangelism" with "The Bridge to Life"

Another easy tool is called "The Bridge" from a discipleship ministry called The Navigators.[1] For a demonstration of how to use this bridge, watch my four-minute video, *Bridge Gospel Illustration.*[2] The idea is to use the following verse and create an illustration so you can explain the gospel:

> For the wages of sin is death, but the gift of God is eternal life in Christ Jesus our Lord. (Rom. 6:23)

Write out this verse on top of a piece of paper. Then begin with something like the following: "Imagine you're standing on one side of a cliff, and you're separated by a huge chasm from the other side. You can see the other side, but there doesn't seem to be any way to get across this abyss. If you fall, you'll be gone forever. This is how it is with our relationship with God. Although God loves us, our sins have separated us from him *relationally.* Scripture says, 'But your iniquities have separated you from your God; your sins have hidden his face from you, so that he will not hear'" (Isa. 59:2).

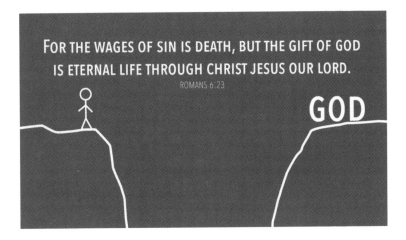

FOR THE WAGES OF SIN IS DEATH, BUT THE GIFT OF GOD IS ETERNAL LIFE THROUGH CHRIST JESUS OUR LORD.
ROMANS 6:23

GOD

The first question to ask them is how they get to the other side. The obvious answer is that they need a bridge. Looking at the first part of Romans 6:23, "For the *wages* of *sin* is *death*," circle each key word as you discuss what they mean as explained below.

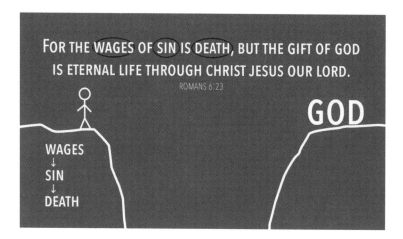

- *Wages.* "What is a wage? A wage is something we earn in exchange for work we have done. When you put in work for your company, you earn money in exchange. What would you think if your boss refused to pay you for all the work you put in?"

- *Sin.* "What comes to mind when you think of sin? Sin is anything we say, think, or do that is not pleasing to God. It involves actions and our hidden intentions. It includes our selfish inclinations contrary to God."

- *Death.* "Death is both physical and spiritual. There is no getting around it. There's a 100 percent chance you're going to die. 'It is appointed for everyone to die once, and after this comes the judgment' (Heb. 9:27)."

This step is important, because if the person doesn't have any concept of being a sinner and the consequences (wages) of their sins, then they may not appreciate the gift of salvation that Jesus freely offers.

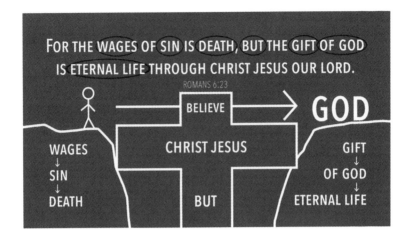

Then finish your presentation by emphasizing the cross, which is the bridge. This shows we can never reach God on our own—not by our own good works or religion. Next say, "Now you've heard the bad news, *but* God has good news for you!" Circle the word *but* in the middle of Romans 6:23, "*But the gift of God* is *eternal life* in *Christ Jesus our Lord*," and then discuss each of the following words as you circle them:

- *Gift.* "If wages are what a person earns, then what is a gift?" They'll say it's something given. Affirm their answer and then stress the importance of this concept. "What would you think if you spent several months savings to buy a diamond ring for your fiancée; but after your proposal, she opened up her purse and handed you a stack of hundred-dollar bills to pay for the ring?" Listen to their response as you reemphasize this being a gift!

- *Of God.* Explain how this gift is from God himself. "Can you remember when someone you truly respected or loved gave you a special gift? How did that make you feel?"

- *Eternal Life.* How would you define eternal life? Contrast one side of the cliff (death), with the other side (eternal life).

"What is the opposite of death?" and "How would you like to receive eternal life?"

- *Christ Jesus.* Write these words to create a bridge between the two cliffs. Help your friend consider that just as every gift has a unique giver, only Jesus Christ can give the gift of eternal life. You can then explain that Jesus is "the only way to the Father" (John 14:6); he is our only bridge across the great divide to God (1 Tim. 2:5). Jesus said, "I tell you the truth, whoever hears my word and believes him who sent me has eternal life and will not be judged. He has crossed over from death unto life" (John 5:24). "Would you like to receive God's free gift of eternal life by placing your faith in Jesus right now?"

Three Diagnostic Questions

A third simple tool of evangelism is to ask questions that allow a person to discover their need of the good news. When I'm talking to an atheist or unbeliever, this is one of the first questions I ask: "If you discovered Christianity was true, would you become a Christian?"

This question gets at the heart as to whether this person is really seeking the truth or if they just want to hold on to a set of beliefs that will allow them to live however they want, with no moral authority to hold them accountable one day. Since atheists frequently claim to be motivated by that which is intellectual, scientific, and verifiable, some of them will say, "Yes, I'd become a Christian." But I've also heard atheists tell me, "Even if Christianity was true, I still would not become a Christian." Notice how absurd it is for someone who claims to be rational to admit they would not believe something even if they knew it was *true.* That's as willfully ignorant as refusing a cure for cancer if you knew you could be healed.

Thomas Nagel, an eminent philosopher at New York University, America's highest ranked program of philosophy, said,

I speak from experience, being strongly subject to this fear myself: I want atheism to be true and am made uneasy by the fact that some of the most intelligent and well-informed people I know are religious believers. It isn't just that I don't believe in God and, naturally, hope that I'm right in my belief. It's that I hope there is no God! I don't want there to be a God; I don't want the universe to be like that.[3]

Professor Nagel admits he *wants* atheism to be true, and says that his colleagues in academia think the same way. He then concludes that disdain toward the idea of God actually existing has influenced many professors holding the "ludicrous overuse of evolutionary biology to explain everything about human life." So, if a person admits that they wouldn't believe something even if it is true, you could then ask, "How do you define truth? And how important is truth to you?" You might ask, "Do you believe that the truth about reality is knowable?" If they answer no, you could ask, "How do you *know* that?" and then, smiling, see if they catch that they just made a self-refuting statement.

If you discover that someone considers themselves a spiritual or religious person, you could ask questions to gauge what they depend on for their salvation. The late minister from Florida, D. James Kennedy, used two "diagnostic questions" to stimulate a spiritual conversation with an unbeliever:

1. On a scale from 1–10, if you were to die today, how certain are you that you would go to heaven? (1 being the least sure to 10 being absolutely certain.)

2. Suppose that you were to die today and stand before God, and he were to say to you, "Why should I let you into my heaven?" What would you say?[4]

These questions are good because they get people thinking about the afterlife. Muslims believe their salvation is based on works, and they often fear they haven't obeyed Allah and the teaching of the prophet Mohammed enough, so many of them aren't sure they are going to heaven.

There are also many professing Christians who grew up going to church but are counting on their good works or church attendance for salvation. You can allow these diagnostic questions to help that person discover if they are trusting in their own works for salvation or in the work of Christ on the cross.

Of course, there are some religions and atheists who don't believe in heaven. Here are some questions you can ask them: "So when you die, what do you think is on the other side?" or "There are some agnostics who affirm a reality of a transcendent soul. What about you? Do you believe humans have an immaterial soul that lives on after the body dies?" We'll talk about atheists later in this book, but it's helpful to use these good "diagnostic" questions from Pastor Kennedy.

Each person on earth is a unique individual, and therefore no single gospel presentation will be perfectly effective to persuade every individual. Being imperfect ourselves, it's natural that we can give only an imperfect presentation of our perfect Savior! But these three tools—the Romans Road, the Bridge, and the Three Diagnostic Questions—have been used for decades to lead millions of souls around the world to a saving knowledge of Jesus Christ. If we take the time to memorize Scripture and learn a few simple tools, God can use us much more effectively in helping spread the good news about Jesus.

6

HELPING PEOPLE UNDERSTAND
THE SIN PROBLEM

Before we can receive the good news, we need to understand that there is a problem: We have *sinned* against a holy and righteous God. Many of us struggle with low self-esteem, while others tend to think too highly of ourselves morally and assume that God "accepts us just the way we are."

As we engage in Jesus Conversations, how then can we communicate that every one of us is intrinsically valuable, created and loved by God; and yet we are all sinners separated from God due to our rebellion against him. If we can recognize this and repent, then we can be saved through Jesus' death on the cross and rise to new life at the Last Day. If we don't repent and turn in faith to Jesus, then we condemn ourselves to God's judgment on that Last Day. In this chapter, we will look at two useful tools: the Ten Commandments and the natural law written on our hearts. These will help people to look more honestly at their faulty mind-set and perhaps see more clearly their need for a Savior.

My friend Nanette told me that when sharing the gospel with her neighbor, she had a difficult time helping her neighbor understand that she was a *sinner* who had committed wrongdoings against a perfectly just God. Have you ever had a similar conversation when a person—who may even be familiar with Christianity—believes that God "accepts us the way we are" and that to mention sin would be "throwing stones"?

Let's consider this question. *Does* God accept us just the way we are? We know the answer depends on the meaning of "accept." Just because Jesus asks us to come to him as we are doesn't mean that God *approves* of everything we do! In fact, God tells us in his word that he loves us so much he wants to change us. Paul told the church at Rome that "those who God foreknew, he chose them to be transformed [changed!] to be like his Son" (Rom. 8:29).

My father is a pastor and Christian school teacher in Staunton, Virginia. He once engaged in an interesting conversation with a young woman in a coffee shop near Mary Baldwin College, a local university known for its liberal leanings. Sitting at a nearby table, she overheard my dad's conversation with another man about their church. "Would your church accept me?" she asked loudly, interrupting them.

My father noticed her rainbow-colored shirt that read *Virginia is for ALL Lovers*, quickly realizing she was an advocate of LGBTQ rights. It seemed she was looking for an argument. Instead of immediately launching into this controversial topic of same-sex relationships, my dad calmly responded, "You would certainly be welcome to visit our church."

After learning the young woman's name, he asked, "I noticed your bright rainbow shirt and I'm curious: wouldn't you agree with me that everybody in the world wants to experience *true* love?"

She responded, "Yes, of course."

My dad replied, "If you decide to come not just to our church but to the person of Jesus Christ, you will discover a dimension of love that is far greater and more wonderful than anything you've ever imagined! And, secondly, if you come to Jesus, he is in the *changing business*, because he wants to make us more like himself. He has changed my friend and me here, and I can tell you that all his changes are for good!"

By this time, she had heard enough and turned away. Notice that my dad did not harp on her same-sex advocacy but turned the conversation to Christ and how Jesus changes all of us. As we engage in Jesus Conversations, we can't skip the fact that coming to Christ involves *change*. The biblical word *repentance* basically means "to turn, to change," and this will sometimes mean a radical change in one's life—but it will all ultimately be for good! Sadly, many in our culture embrace a false spirituality that acknowledges the existence of God but denies moral absolutes, the existence of sin, and any need to repent (that is, change). There is a large emphasis of "love" in our society, but rarely any mention of sin.

In philosophy, the term "ontology" speaks of the nature of our being, our existence, and what it means to be a human person. As human beings, we are "ontologically" good, meaning that every single one of us is intrinsically priceless, made in the very image of God. Paul tells us that "we are God's masterpiece" (Eph. 2:10 NLT). So, when speaking about your essence, the fact that you are a human being who exists means you are highly valuable just the way you are! In fact, you're so valuable that God through the person of Jesus died for you. Scripture is clear that as God's creation, you are "very good" (Gen. 1) and that you are "fearfully and wonderfully made" (Ps. 139).

But because humanity disobeyed God, sin came into this world and thus *morally* we are evil. Ontologically, in our essence, we are very good. Morally, we are wicked and rebellious against God. This is known as the doctrine of "depravity." Depravity is a word that means moral corruption and wickedness. In our culture, we downplay our sins with phrases like "I made a mistake," "It was inappropriate behavior," or "I'm struggling," but sin is far more seriously wicked. Sin is a nature and behavior that rebels against God. The Bible makes it clear that we are all depraved. Paul told the church at Rome, "For *all* have sinned and fall short of the glory of God" (Rom. 3:23). In Romans 3:10–12, Paul quotes other Scriptures from the Old Testament (Pss. 14:1–3; 53:1–3; Eccl. 7:20) to explain his case:

> "None is righteous, no, not one;
>   no one understands;
>   no one seeks for God.

All have turned aside;
    together they have become worthless;
no one does good,
    not even one."

The problems in the world today are *not caused primarily* by economic or political issues; the root cause is a *heart problem*. In our essential natures, we are *not* kind and benevolent; instead, we are self-centered and evil. The prophet Jeremiah wrote an apt description of the human heart: "The heart is deceitful above all things, and it is exceedingly perverse *and* corrupt and severely, mortally sick! Who can know it [perceive, understand, be acquainted with his own heart and mind]?" (Jer. 17:9 AMP).

The Ten Commandments Help Us Discover Our Own Evil

When I was in college, I met evangelist Ray Comfort, who effectively appealed to the law, God's Ten Commandments revealed to Moses, to allow a person to understand that they have committed specific sins against a just and holy God. I mentioned in the first chapter that I used a method similar to this at the restaurant to the rap group. This method is beneficial for people who are a little familiar with some religions like Christianity, Islam, or Judaism, which believe there is a God who governs the moral laws of our universe. This is how this method works. If you were engaging in spiritual conversations with an unbeliever, your conversation might look like the following conversation.

"Do you know any of the Ten Commandments?" (They might not know any, so you may need to tell the story of the Ten Commandments, which reflect natural laws that are written on our hearts.)

"I know one," the person may answer. "Thou shalt not murder."

"Yes, God's law says, 'Thou shalt not murder.' Did you know that Jesus said, "If you are even angry with someone, you have committed murder in your heart, and you'll be held accountable! . . . And if you curse someone, you are in danger of the fires of hell"? (Matt. 5:22 NLT). Have you ever hated someone in your heart?"

"Yes."

"What does that make you?"

"A sinner." They may say the word *sinner* to sound spiritual or to try to emphasize back to you that they understand what sin actually is.

"Yes, but specifically, what does that make you?"

They may admit, "A murderer in my heart."

Now at this point, you can mention another commandment or teaching from Jesus in his famous Sermon on the Mount. "Jesus also said, 'You have heard the commandment that says, 'You must not commit adultery.' But I say, anyone who even looks at a woman with lust has already committed adultery with her in his heart" (Matt. 5:28). You might act boldly and ask this person, "Have you ever had lust in your heart or with your eyes?"

With a sheepish grin on their face, they will likely say, "Yes."

"Based on God's commands, would you consider yourself guilty or perfectly innocent?" Pause and let them answer. Then say, "Based on your admission of guilt before God, do you think you will spend your eternal destiny in heaven or hell?" If they say hell, then share the good news!

Notice the sequence of this methodology. At some point in the conversation, you can ask the person if they're familiar with the famous Ten Commandments and if they know what sin is. If they're not familiar with them, you may need to define the words for them. Some Christians say we should completely avoid theological and biblical words, just because some may not know them. Instead, I say, start with common language and then take your time when you introduce a theological word like *sin*. Ask questions and define the word to make sure the person understands what you are talking about.

After you've mentioned the Ten Commandments, ask them if they have broken one of God's commands or Jesus' further clarification of these moral principles in his Sermon on the Mount, in which Jesus gets at the heart of the matter, if we have "committed adultery or murder *in our hearts.*" Then have them admit that they are a specific type of sinner: an adulterer, a blasphemer for taking God's name in vain, a liar, and so on. After their admission, ask the spiritual seeker a question: "Are you guilty or innocent?" Let them answer, and then ask them the second question: "If you are guilty, will you spend eternity in heaven or hell?" If they say heaven based on their pride, you may consider drawing the bridge analogy we discussed in chapter 5, using Romans 6:23 to help them understand the seriousness of their sin.

The Reality of Hell

When asking a person if they would be guilty or innocent on the day of judgment before a holy and just God, we must be urgent and unashamed to speak of the reality of a literal place called hell. No person is recorded in the Bible as speaking and emphasizing the reality of hell as much as Jesus. In over twenty recorded occasions in the New Testament, Jesus likened hell to a place of fire—*twenty* times!

For those who want to say that the Old Testament is all about judgment and the New Testament is only about love and no judgment, then they are hugely mistaken. To people who were engaging in sexual lustful thoughts, Jesus said, "If your right eye causes you to sin, gouge it out and throw it away. It is better for you to lose one part of your body than for your whole body to be thrown into hell. And if your right hand causes you to sin, cut it off and throw it away. It is better for you to lose one part of your body than for your whole body to depart into hell" (Matt. 5:29–30). Jesus also compared hell to Gehenna, a small valley in Jerusalem where some evil kings of Judah sacrificed their children by fire. Because of this wicked act, Gehenna was cursed by God and became the destination of the wicked. Jesus also said that hell was a place of "outer darkness" where there is "weeping and gnashing of teeth" (Matt. 8:12; 13:42, 50; 25:23). In the final book of the Bible, Revelation, Jesus says:

> "I am the Alpha and the Omega, the Beginning and the End. To the thirsty I will give water without cost from the spring of the water of life. Those who are victorious will inherit all this, and I will be their God and they will be my children. But the cowardly, the unbelieving, the vile, the murderers, the sexually immoral, those who practice magic arts, the idolaters and all liars—they will be consigned to the fiery lake of burning sulfur. This is the second death." (Rev. 21:6-8)

If the person you're witnessing to claims to be a "spiritual person" or even a Christian and they don't believe in hell, you may ask them to read a short passage such as Revelation 21:6-8 and ask, "Do you believe this is true? Will you spend eternity in heaven or hell?"

"Right for You, but Not Right for Me."

When discussing religion or morality, we might hear someone say something like the following: "That may be right for you, but it's not right for me. Don't impose your bigoted religious morals on me." This is the philosophical term known as "moral relativism." Some people don't believe there's anything that is objectively morally wrong or evil, that these are just "social constructs."

If the person is a professing atheist who grew up going to church, they may even mock you by quoting the Law of Moses. I have heard atheists say, "Do you ever wear clothing made of two kinds of material? Because Leviticus [19:19] forbids that too!" Now, you could go down some rabbit trail, but I would encourage you to simply say, "We both know that some of the Mosaic law was ceremonial and purely descriptive for a particular people in Israel's history. Let's agree with that. Can we also agree that some moral principles are absolutely wrong for all people at all times and all places? For example, is there anywhere in the world, where it is morally good for an adult man to rape a seven-year-old girl?"

Another good question to ask an atheist is this: "What is the basis of your morality?" If they try to say that morality is relative, then pick an obvious example: "In today's media, there's a lot of attention on women who have been sexually abused in the workplace. Do you think these actions toward women are just 'relatively wrong' or are they *actually wrong*?" Most moral relativists will start contradicting themselves very quickly. They may not admit there is a real right and wrong, but you will soon hear them saying things like, "That's not right" or "I have rights!"

The Natural Law Written on Men's Hearts

When I was visiting Manhattan, I asked a young professional man why he didn't believe in God. He told me that he grew up Catholic and despised the evil things priests and religious leaders did, including molesting children. After asking questions about the laws of nature, physics, and science, I listened to him give an explanation for why he believed only in science and evolution.

I then asked him, "Is evil real?"

He said, "No, evil is just a social construct. What may be evil for you may not be evil for me. It's all relative."

"Are you sure about that? Everything is just 'relatively' good or evil?" He had completely forgotten what he told me earlier about the Catholic Church and his reasons for rejecting the faith, so I told him point-blank, "Maybe we should just end this conversation if you think that when a wicked priest molests a child, it's only relatively evil!" I started to walk away, and he smiled because he knew I had caught him contradicting himself. Although he didn't convert to Christ during this short conversation, he moved from being an atheist to an open-minded agnostic who was willing to close his eyes and pray with me in public.

There are many pastors who argue that we should completely avoid talking about controversial issues such as abortion, sexuality, or gender, thinking that if they just proclaim a message of love and affirmation, more unbelievers will come to the faith. But in Scripture, we see a message of both love and repentance of sin. When an agnostic or a person of a different religion recognizes they have sinned, they may be open to the idea of atonement.

On one occasion, I was asked to speak at an open forum art outreach in Uptown Dallas. At the time, I was traveling the country giving talks at pregnancy center banquets and universities on the sacredness of human life. When my friend, Frank Bonilla, asked me to give the keynote talk, I told him I was busy speaking on the pro-life/abortion debate and didn't have time to create another talk on such a short notice. But Frank said, "That's fine! I just want you to speak."

Since I didn't have to prepare anything, I agreed and spoke at the outreach for fifteen minutes on "You Are God's Masterpiece: Why All Humans are Sacred." I talked about how those of all faiths know there is something intrinsically valuable and beautiful about human beings. I started by finding common ground with the audience and talked about how our children attend schools with zero-tolerance policies for violence; our celebrities regularly take to the airwaves to discourage bullying; and not only do we arrest and publicly eviscerate anyone found to be involved in animal abuse such as dog fighting, but improperly handling the egg of a bald eagle is punishable with up to a $250,000 fine and six months in prison. I asked, "Surely a society that condemns violence of any kind would be free from man-made epidemics of death?"

I continued, "But since Supreme Court's *Roe v. Wade* decision in 1973—which, along with *Doe v. Bolton*, effectively made it illegal to restrict abortion at any stage of pregnancy—more than 60 million American babies have died from being aborted. To this day, we continue to lose more than 1.2 million a year: our own killing fields, our own genocide, our own holocaust."

I looked at the audience of artists and said, "According to pro-choice activists who disagree with me, these 60 million babies would have been born into horrible circumstances or prevented their mothers from realizing important life goals. Their lives, we are to believe, were not worth living. But have the deaths of these babies really improved the lives of their mothers and fathers, or have they left an unmistakable mark?"

As I paused and looked at the audience, I noticed there was a young man in his twenties in the second row with tears streaming down his face. It was evident his emotions were stirred toward the truth he was hearing. After my talk, his friend explained to me that earlier this week he had been suicidal from the guilt and shame of taking his girlfriend to get an abortion at Planned Parenthood.

Compelled to comfort him, I sat down to his left. I felt moved to share the hope of the gospel with him. After a few moments of getting acquainted, I began to lead him in prayer. Repeating after my words, he began proclaiming the love of Jesus Christ and his need of a Savior. He repeated after me, "Cleanse me with the blood of Jesus Christ." After we prayed, I looked him in his eyes and reminded him, "There is now no condemnation for those who are in Christ Jesus. Jesus has set you free from sin and death." Not long after, I was surprise to discover that this young man who prayed to trust Jesus for the first time was actually a Muslim. You see, it was the topic of abortion and the sacredness of human life that allowed this young man to be open to the solution of Christ's cleansing blood on the cross and resurrected life, even having Islamic influence in his life.

When we talk about sins such as abortion, even people of other faiths may feel convicted, because it violates the law that God has written on their hearts. Paul the Apostle talked about this natural law to the church at Rome:

> Even Gentiles, who do not have God's written law, show that they know his law when they instinctively obey it, even without having heard it. They demonstrate that God's law is written

in their hearts, for their own conscience and thoughts either accuse them or tell them they are doing right. And this is the message I proclaim—that the day is coming when God, through Christ Jesus, will judge everyone's secret life. (Rom. 2:14–16)

We can therefore appeal to the "law" written on our hearts. This is what Jesus did in his conversation with the woman at the well in John 4. When he told her to go get her husband, she said, "I have no husband." He then said, "You are right when you say you have no husband. You have had five husbands, and the man you are living with now is not your husband. What you have said is quite true." Notice how Jesus appealed to the law written on her heart without quoting the Old Testament.

If someone denies the reality of objective moral law, listen to them. You might hear a contradiction or they'll say, "You shouldn't impose your view on me." Then you may ask them, "What do you mean by 'shouldn't'? Doesn't that mean 'should not' as in a moral imperative? In other words, is there an action I should not do—namely, impose my view on you? But haven't you done the same thing by imposing your view on me that I shouldn't impose my view on you?"

As we listen to such critics, we can say, "Help me understand: Is it ever all right to impose one's moral view on another?" You might add, "Perhaps we could find some common ground. If we saw a man physically abusing a child in public, shouldn't we impose our view on him, tell him to stop, and then call law enforcement?" These types of questions may help the person discover that they really do believe some things are right and some are really wrong.

Because of the denial of moral absolutes and the authority of the Bible, it is vital for Christians to understand both the Ten Commandments and that there is natural law written on the heart that reflects the principles of these commandments.

7

Seven Truths of the Gospel

As we emphasized in the last section, acknowledging sin is a prerequisite to understanding the gospel. Before a person hears the "good news," they need to understand the "bad news." As we've already mentioned, the word *gospel* means good news! While explaining this good news, however, there are seven key points to keep in mind. Although you may not need to talk about all seven every time you engage in a spiritual conversation, it is helpful to memorize the basics of these truths.

When you are working on these seven truths of the gospel, you may want to memorize verses that accompany these doctrines and also practice explaining them in your own words. So, attempting to avoid being too narrow or too broad, here are "seven truths" one must believe about the gospel:

1. *God* exists and he created everything.

2. Jesus is fully *God*.

3. Jesus is fully *man*.

4. Jesus *died* for our sins.

5. Jesus *rose* from the dead.

6. Salvation is a gift of God's *grace*.

7. Salvation is given to those who respond in *faith*.

In chapter 5, we talked about using the "Bridge" analogy and the "Romans Road," but sometimes you can just include these seven truths of the gospel. Work on a way you can use these truths in your own words when having a Jesus Conversation. After starting a conversation, asking questions, and listening to the person, you might ask, "Is it all right for me to share with you what I believe?" You could say something like this: "I believe that God exists and that he created the entire universe. Adam and Eve, the first humans, disobeyed God. Because of their sin, brokenness and death came into the world." At this point, you could ask, "Do you agree that the world we live in is *broken*?" Most people will agree with you.

You can then continue by saying something like the following: "Since the beginning of our existence, we humans have been disobeying God and hurting one another both physically and emotionally. Our world is broken, and we have tried to fix that brokenness with religion, education, science, relationships, health, and comfort. These things are good, but the brokenness in our world still exists, and none of them will ever restore our relationship with God. God is perfectly just and holy, and he demands justice. But out of his love, God through the person of Jesus entered into humanity and became like us in our world over two thousand years ago. He lived a perfect life that we could have never lived and died in our place on the cross. Three days later, Jesus rose from the dead, proving his deity. He appeared to many people. He now offers salvation to anyone who believes in him and repents of their sin. This salvation is a gift received through faith, and it is not by our good works. He is coming back soon."

As you memorize the seven fundamental doctrinal truths, practice with a small group by putting them in your own words and being conversational. Although you may not say them the same way every time, it's important that you memorize them correctly.

While we're thinking theologically about what the gospel actually is, I'd like to explain in further detail the biblical basis for these doctrines and the passages of Scripture that correlate with them. These doctrinal truths are unlikely to come up in detail during every conversation, but it critical for Christians to know how and *why* this is the gospel.

Core Truth #1: God *Exists* and He *Created* Everything

The late theologian R. C. Sproul was once asked, "What is the difference between the Christian God and the gods of other religions?" Sproul noted the main difference is this: "The God of Christianity exists."[1] One of God's attributes is existence. He is *real*. When I've asked Christians if God is real and they respond yes, I then ask them why they think that. Their response is usually, "Because I have faith." This answer, however, is absolutely false.

Now, of course, we may come to a relational *knowledge* that God is real through the inward witness of the Holy Spirit, and therefore we place our faith in him. But God is not real because somebody has faith. That's heresy! Rather, *because God is real*, we should therefore place our faith in him. The writer of the book of Hebrews says, "Without faith, it is impossible to please God, because anyone who comes to him must believe *that he exists* and that he rewards those who earnestly seek him" (Heb. 11:6; my italics). Notice that the text indicates that one has a simple belief *in God's existence* before coming to God in faith, resulting in salvation.

Do you remember when God revealed himself to Moses in the book of Exodus? Before God created the universe, he *existed*. God told Moses that his name is "I Am." As humans, we have not always existed. There must be a being who is self-existent and necessary, and not dependent upon anything else for his existence. This being is God, who revealed himself to Moses as "I Am."

Second, it is important to note that some religions believe God is everything, such as pantheism. Pantheistic religions—such as Hinduism and some forms of Buddhist spirituality—say that God *is everything* and that life's purpose is to understand your oneness with that reality. But this doctrine is false. Christianity doesn't teach that God is everything, but rather that God *made* everything. This is vital for you to know when you're sharing the gospel with your neighbor who is a Hindu, a Buddhist, or a friend who is interested in yoga's spiritual teaching, new age mysticism, neopaganism, or self-help spirituality. If you don't articulate the reality that the God of Christianity *exists* and that God *created* everything and is distinct from the universe, they may say they are "fine" with Jesus and "accept Jesus" but not take him seriously. They'll just "add" him to the figment of their spiritual imagination.

When Paul and Barnabas were doing miracles in the name of Jesus, the crowds in Asia Minor were amazed and said, "The gods have come down." But Paul and Barnabas harshly rebuked them and said,

> "Men, why are you doing these things? We also are men, of like nature with you, and we bring you good news, that you should turn from these vain things to a living God, who made the heaven and the earth and the sea and all that is in them."
>
> (Acts 14:15)

Notice several key points in this passage. First, Paul and Barnabas rebuked the people for their false beliefs. Second, Paul affirmed that they too were men, with the same nature as other people. Paul was clearly teaching that God has a nature or being that is different from humans. Third, Paul was saying, "I bring you good news," which is the same Greek term for "gospel." This gospel is that they should turn to a living God, who is the one who made the heaven, the earth, and the sea. It is therefore critical to include in the gospel that God is the real, living God and that he created everything, including the universe (which consists of the heavens, the earth, the sea, and so on).

Here is a key verse to meditate on and memorize:

> For since the creation of the world God's invisible qualities—his eternal power and divine nature—have been clearly seen,

being understood from what has been made, so that people are without excuse. (Rom. 1:20)

Core Truth #2: Jesus Is Fully *God*

Have you ever talked to someone who denied that Jesus was God? Whenever you proclaim the gospel to Muslims, Jehovah's Witnesses, or Mormons who deny the deity of Jesus, you'll need to be familiar with Scriptures that explain that Jesus is God. We know that at the birth of Jesus, the angels declared the gospel (good news!) that Jesus is the Christ, the Lord's Anointed:

> The angel said to them, "Fear not, for behold, I bring you good news of great joy that will be for all the people. For unto you is born this day in the city of David a Savior, who is Christ the Lord." (Luke 2:10–11)

The gospel is centered on Jesus. John, a close disciple of Jesus and an eyewitness, described Jesus as the Word eternally existing with God the Father:

> In the beginning was the Word, and the Word was with God, and the Word was God. He was with God in the beginning. Through him all things were made; without him, nothing was made that has been made. (John 1:1–3)

Notice how John says that the Word was with God and also *was God*. John then adds,

> The Word became flesh and made his dwelling among us. We have seen his glory, the glory of the one and only Son, who came from the Father, full of grace and truth. (John 1:14)

This means that in the incarnation, the being conceived in the womb of the Virgin Mary is the Second Person of the Trinity, eternally God, who takes on a human nature. The Second Person of the Trinity, who has always been God, took on human flesh and was born at a specific time and place in history. He was named Jesus, which means "Jehovah saves" (or Yeshua, "Yahweh saves"). Jesus understood himself to be God and did only those things that Yahweh, the living God, can do. The Jewish disciples of Jesus were familiar with what God said through the prophet Isaiah,

> "When you pass through the waters, I will be with you; and when you pass through the rivers, they will not sweep over you." (Isa. 43:2)

Jesus revealed himself as this living God when his disciples were afraid that they would die during the storm. Jesus, proving he was God, walked on water! On another occasion, Jesus calmed a horrific storm by saying, "Be quiet!" Can you imagine being his disciples? At one moment you think you're going to die, but then you hear Jesus rebuke the storm. Wow! Scripture says, "The men were amazed and asked, 'What kind of man is this? Even the winds and the waves obey him!'" (Matt. 8:27).

Jesus understood himself to be God and claimed to be the "Son of Man seated at the right hand of Power, and coming with the clouds of heaven" (Mark 14:62). The "Son of Man" was not just a reference to Christ's humanity, but it was also his Messianic deity as described by the prophet Daniel in which "all peoples, nations, and languages should serve him" (Dan. 7:14). Jesus also claimed to be "I Am," which is the name God used to reveal himself to Moses (John 8:58). Most telling: Jesus' extraordinary claims to be equivalent with God caused the Jews to accuse him of blasphemy and want to kill him.

> For this reason, the Jews tried all the harder to kill him; not only was he breaking the Sabbath, but he was even calling God his own Father, making himself *equal* with God. (John 5:18; my italics)

The word *equal* in Greek should leave no doubt of Jesus' claims. Many other Scriptures also attest to Jesus' deity.[2]

Here is a key verse to meditate on and memorize:

> So the Jews said to him, "You are not yet fifty years old, and have you seen Abraham?" Jesus said to them, "Truly, truly, I say to you, before Abraham was, I am." (John 8:57–58 ESV)

Core Truth #3: Jesus Is Fully *Man*

For a sacrifice sufficient to forgive all the sins of all people, the sacrifice has to be perfect; but as only God is perfect, therefore God alone must be the perfect sacrifice. But the sacrifice was for humans, and therefore the sacrifice had to be *fully human* as well. The humanity of Christ is thus necessary for salvation. In orthodox Christianity, we're taught that it is a heresy to deny Christ's full humanity. This heresy is known as Docetism, which denies that Jesus came as a real man, that he only *appeared* to be human. Docetism comes from a Greek word that means "apparition, illusion, or phantom." Bishop Serapion of Antioch (197–203) was an early church leader who used the word *docetai* (illusionist) to refer to those groups, such as the gnostics, that denied Jesus' humanity. In Christian circles, this is talked about less frequently than other heresies, but it is still relevant and important to recognize today.

Some professing Christians subconsciously embrace a "Jesus of the heart," but their "Jesus" may be distinct from the "Jesus of history." In other words, these people don't believe it's necessary that Jesus lived historically as a real man who died on the cross, so long as he "lives in one's heart" and they can feel some sort of experience of the sentimental feelings of spirituality or relationship with God. The apostle Paul warned about embracing "another Jesus" (i.e., a counterfeit Jesus) and accepting a "different gospel" (2 Cor. 11:4).

For example, many liberal ministers—such as American Episcopal Church bishop John Shelby Spong—reject the historical reliability of the gospel, the virgin birth, the crucifixion, and bodily resurrection of Jesus, but they believe in "personal spirituality." We have seen this type of teaching increase in our culture, which has shifted to emphasize a "personal relationship" with Jesus while de-emphasizing history, doctrine, and facts. It is therefore critical that we proclaim the realness and humanity of Jesus in history.

How shall we respond? Does Jesus want a personal relationship? Of course! The Jesus of history is the Jesus of my heart. Jesus is real, he came in the flesh, and his Spirit living in me should be my confession. The doctrine of Jesus coming to earth in the flesh was emphasized by Paul, Peter, and John. When some of Jesus' disciples saw him, they were scared and thought he was a ghost. He rebuked them and then proved that he had a body, albeit a resurrected one:

> He showed them his hands and feet. And while they still did not believe it because of joy and amazement, he asked them, "Do you have anything here to eat?" They gave him a piece of broiled fish, and he took it and ate it in their presence. (Luke 24:40–43)

Here's a key verse to meditate on and memorize:

> Dear friends, do not believe every spirit but test the spirits to see whether they are from God because many false prophets have gone out into the world. This is how you can recognize the Spirit of God: Every spirit that acknowledges *that Jesus Christ has come in the flesh* is from God. (1 John 4:1–2; my italics)

Core Truth #4: Jesus *Died* for Our Sins

The fourth truth of the gospel that must be proclaimed is the death of Jesus. The mission of Jesus coming to earth was to *die* for our sins. God is holy and demands perfect justice. But out of love, he took our punishment for us, through the person of Jesus. Paul said,

God presented Christ as a sacrifice of atonement, through the shedding of his blood—to be received by faith. (Rom. 3:25)

When Paul was writing to the believers in Corinth, he wanted to emphasize the truths of what the gospel is and remind them of what they already knew:

> Now I would tell you, brothers, of the gospel I preached to you, which you received, in which you stand, and by which you are being saved if you hold fast to the word I preached to you— unless you believed in vain. For I delivered to you as of first importance what I also received: that Christ died for our sins in accordance with the Scriptures, that he was buried, that he was raised on the third day in accordance with the Scriptures, and that he appeared to Cephas, then to the twelve. Then he appeared to more than five hundred brothers at one time, most of whom are still alive, though some have fallen asleep. Then he appeared to James, then to all the apostles. (1 Cor. 15:1–7 ESV)

The centrality of the gospel rests in the historical fact that Jesus Christ died on the cross for our sins. Although Muslims deny that Jesus historically died on the cross, the essence of our Christian faith must be that Christ the Savior did *die*. To be an effective everyday evangelist, it's good for you to be able to provide some reasons of how we know that Jesus died in history. We will discuss this below under Core Truth #5.

Paul said, "We preach Christ crucified, a stumbling block to Jews and folly to Gentiles" (1 Cor. 1:23 ESV). Even John Dominic Crossan, a liberal scholar of the Jesus Seminar, said the truth of Jesus' crucifixion "is as sure as anything historical can be."[3] The Romans were experts in execution. They made sure they got the job done, or they were severely punished. When you read the Scriptures, always remember that Jesus endured the fatal torment of the cross for you and even for that neighbor, coworker, or relative who gets under your skin and annoys you. Jesus loves them and died for all of us.

Paul reminds the church of the essentials of the gospel: the death, burial, and resurrection of Jesus Christ; and if we believe this message, we can be saved from our sins. Many scholars think the account of the resurrection appearances of Jesus in the 1 Corinthians 15 passage cited above is an early pre-Pauline creedal statement. When sharing the gospel with a Muslim or someone who does not believe that Jesus historically died, you will have confidence in knowing that the earliest historical sources mention Jesus and speak of his death and resurrection.

Here's a key verse to meditate on and memorize:

> For I delivered to you as of first importance what I also received: that Christ died for our sins in accordance with the Scriptures, that he was buried, that he was raised on the third day in accordance with the Scriptures, and that he appeared to Cephas, then to the twelve. Then he appeared to more than five hundred brothers at one time. (1 Cor. 15:3–4)

Core Truth #5: Jesus *Rose* from the Dead

As I mentioned earlier, I once asked a pastor friend of mind how he would summarize the essentials of the gospel. He talked about God loving the world and Jesus dying for our sins. He also explained how this good news is by God's grace, not by works. But he completely forgot to mention the resurrection of Jesus!

The resurrection of Jesus is essential and cannot be forgotten when articulating the core truths of the gospel. Paul, making a case for the resurrection of Jesus, reminded the church at Corinth that if Christ has not been raised, then "our preaching is useless and so is your faith" (1 Cor. 15:14). He added that if Christ has not been raised from the dead, then "we are of all people most to be pitied" (1 Cor. 15:19).

Below is a helpful way to help you provide evidence for Jesus' resurrection—all by using the letter "e"!

"E" Early Testimony

All four of the Gospels were written in the first century. Matthew and John were two of Jesus' twelve disciples who lived, ate, traveled, and developed a close friendship with him; and Mark and Luke gathered eyewitness testimony and were the companions of those who were eyewitnesses. Also, within Paul's letters, there are creeds that predate the letters Paul writes early in the first century. The *early* creed of 1 Corinthians 15 tells us that the gospel is the death, burial, and resurrection of Jesus.

When I was an undergraduate student at Liberty University, my theology professor, Dr. Gary Habermas, explained how he had researched and cataloged every scholarly article published on the resurrection of Jesus. He concluded, "Essentially all critical scholars today agree that in 1 Corinthians 15:3–8, Paul records an ancient oral tradition(s) that summarizes the content of the Christian gospels."[4] Even the most skeptical scholars agree that the creed in 1 Corinthians 15 was formulated and taught at a date soon after Jesus' death.[5]

"E" Eyewitnesses

One of the fascinating pieces of evidence of the resurrection is the variety of *eyewitness* accounts of the resurrection. In 1 Corinthians 15:6, Paul writes,

> Then he [Jesus] appeared to more than five hundred brothers at one time, most of whom are still alive, though some have fallen asleep.

Notice what Paul is saying: There are more than five hundred eyewitnesses, and most of them were still alive when he wrote this letter. In other words, "If you don't believe me, go ask them for yourselves. They'll tell you they saw Jesus risen from the dead with their own eyes." Not only were John and Matthew eyewitnesses of Jesus, but so were other writers including James and Jude (Jesus' half-brothers), as well as Peter.

"E" Empty Tomb

In the early creed that Paul emphasized to the church at Corinth, another piece of strong evidence of Jesus' resurrection is the *empty tomb* reported in all four canonical Gospel accounts. Papias, in the early second century, said that the Gospel of Mark was "written by John Mark, a companion and interpreter of Peter." Mark's Gospel—which reports the empty tomb—is simple and lacks the legendary embellishment we see in second-century gnostic gospels, which were disproved by the early church and not included in the New Testament canon. If we look at the Gospel of Thomas, where there is a large talking cross and Jesus tells the disciples that Mary needs to make herself a man in order to enter heaven, we can see why the church chose not to include it! It's the same with the other gnostic gospels that didn't make it into the canon.

Mark's Gospel contains internal evidence that it was written by an eyewitness or a contemporary who gathered information from eyewitnesses. The disciple Matthew, a Jewish tax collector employed by Rome, wrote in polished synagogue Greek. John, an eyewitness of the empty tomb, recounts going into the tomb with Peter, where he "bent over and looked in at the strips of linen lying there" (John 20:5). Many witnesses attested to the empty tomb of Jesus.

"E" Embarrassing Details Not Omitted

Another line of evidence—the testimony of women—would have been considered *embarrassing* for men in that culture and time period. In the first-century courts of Palestine, testimony from a woman was considered worthless. The first-century Jewish historian Josephus recorded: "But let not the testimony of women be admitted, on account of the levity and boldness of their sex."[6] Despite this prejudice against women, the Gospel accounts accurately record what happened—namely, that the women were the first to go to the empty tomb and to see the risen Jesus.

In addition, it seems that if the early Christians had fabricated a story about Jesus' resurrection, they wouldn't have recorded the fact that all of the close disciples fled after Jesus was taken captive by the Romans (one of them even ran away naked!), while the brave and courageous women stayed with him at the cross and were the first to show up at the empty tomb.

"E" Excruciating Persecution

After the resurrection, eleven of the twelve apostles suffered and were eventually martyred, not just because of something they "believed in." They were martyred for something they *passionately thought to be true*. Although people may die for a lie they thought was true, they don't die for a lie they know to be false. Peter Kreeft, a philosophy professor at Boston College, says,

> Why would the apostles lie? . . . If they lied, what was their motive, what did they get out of this? What they got out of it was misunderstanding, rejection, persecution, torture, and martyrdom. Hardly a list of perks.[7]

Chuck Colson served as special counsel to President Richard Nixon from 1969 to 1973 and gained notoriety during the Watergate scandal, in which several men broke into the Democratic National Convention headquarters at the Watergate Complex in Washington, DC, on June 17, 1972, in which Richard Nixon's administration attempted to cover up its involvement. Colson later pleaded guilty to obstruction of justice and spent seven months in the federal Maxwell prison in Alabama. In 1973, Colson became a Christian and founded Prison Fellowship, a nonprofit ministry. Speaking at a prison on Easter Sunday 1982, he said,

> I know the resurrection is a fact, and Watergate proved it to me. How? Because 12 men testified they had seen Jesus raised from the dead, then they proclaimed that truth for 40 years, never once denying it. Everyone was beaten, tortured, stoned and put in prison. They would not have endured that if it weren't true. Watergate embroiled 12 of the most powerful men in the world,

and they couldn't keep a lie for three weeks. Are you telling me 12 apostles could keep a lie for 40 years? Absolutely impossible.[8]

The conspiracy alternatives regarding the resurrection that skeptics put forth—such as, the disciples were hallucinating or they stole Jesus' body—lack historical evidence. Although these alternative theories may sound useful to skeptics who seek alternatives, they don't account for the evidence of the *early testimony*, the variety of *eyewitnesses* who saw Jesus after he rose from the dead, the *empty tomb*, the *embarrassing* details that weren't omitted, and the *excruciating persecution of the apostles*.

Core Truth #6: Salvation Is a Gift of God's *Grace*

The sixth truth of the gospel is that it's by God's grace that we are saved and not by our good works. Grace can be defined as God giving us what we do not deserve, while mercy means withholding what we deserve. We are saved by God's grace through the means of faith in Jesus. In Titus 3:5, Paul writes, "He saved us, not because of righteous things we had done, but because of his mercy. He saved us through the washing of rebirth and renewal by the Holy Spirit."

God's grace means that God is giving us a *gift*.

When Paul made the case to the new church in Rome that it was not by works that one is saved, he used Abraham as an example:

> What does Scripture say? "Abraham believed God, and it was credited to him as righteousness." Now to the one who works, wages are not credited as a gift but as an obligation. However, to the one who does not work but trusts God who justifies the ungodly, their faith is credited as righteousness. (Rom. 3:3–5)

So, what is the relationship between works and grace? Well, works are the *effect* of God's grace. When we are changed by the Holy Spirit, it is out of this changed life of walking in obedience that we do good works. Our good works aren't the cause of our salvation;

God's grace is the cause of our salvation, and we receive it through faith in the work of Jesus Christ on the cross.

Here's a key verse to meditate on and memorize:

> For it is by grace you have been saved, through faith—and this is not from yourselves, it is the gift of God—not by works, so that no one can boast. (Eph. 2:8–9)

Core Truth #7: Salvation Is Given to Those Who Respond *in Faith*

The seventh core truth of the gospel is that one must respond to the truths God has revealed and *believe in* Jesus' lordship, death, and resurrection. By "faith," I don't mean a blind leap of faith into something we don't know. Rather, the Greek word for faith (*pistis*) means to trust; it's a response. You and I have a choice to respond to what we know about God, and either trust him or not. As Paul says,

> If you declare with your mouth, "Jesus is Lord," and believe in your heart that God raised him from the dead, you will be saved. For it is with your heart that you believe and are justified, and it is with your mouth that you profess your faith and are saved. (Rom. 10:9–10)

This belief cannot be mere intellectual comprehension *that* Jesus died and rose again, but trusting *in* Jesus that he died for you and bore your sins on the cross. James wrote, "You believe that there is one God. Good! Even the demons believe that—and shudder" (James 2:19). In this case, we know that demons acknowledge the existence of the true God, but they refuse to believe *in* him in a way that leads to obedience. John the Apostle said, "Yet to all who did receive him, to those who believed in his name, he gave the right to become children of God" (John 1:12). With this simple act of believing in Jesus, we also receive him. Let's suppose I told you, "I believe the elevator is trustworthy and will take me floor to floor," yet I continually refuse to use it. Would I be revealing that I genuinely believed the elevator worked? No! But if you saw me step on the elevator and used it, you might conclude I really did believe what I said I did.

Similarly, we must believe in Jesus and place our trust in him. This is an act of surrender. To believe in him as Lord is to affirm his deity and his supremacy. Some theologians differ on whether this belief is simultaneous with *or* immediately followed by repentance. Regardless, you must believe in Jesus and also repent of your sins. The word *repentance* (*metanoia* in Greek) means a changing of one's mind and is commonly translated as "turning away from sin" (Matt. 3:2).

Here's a key verse to meditate on and memorize:

> For God so loved the world that he gave his one and only Son, that whoever believes in him shall not perish but have eternal life. (John 3:16)

There are other truths of the gospel—such as Christ's virgin birth (related to his deity), his ascension, or his bodily return—but I believe these seven are the core essentials we need to know and proclaim when articulating the gospel for salvation.

8

Learning Apologetics

Many of us have a time when we were challenged to not only know *what* we believe but *why we believe* what we believe to be true. For me, that was when I was a senior in high school at Oak Hill Academy. I was a pastor's kid and attended a private evangelical Christian school, but I transferred during my senior year to a private boarding religious school known for being a national powerhouse in basketball. Although my sole intention was to play basketball, looking back, I know the Lord used this as an opportunity to draw me closer to himself. I was required to attend chapel during the week as well as church on Sunday morning. The chaplain and the school staff were extremely kind toward me. But it was in this situation away from home that I faced intellectual challenges toward the truth of what I believed about Christ and the Bible.

One day in chapel, the pastor prayed something like this: "Dear God, some of us call you Father or Jesus, some of us call you Allah, some of us call you other names, but we know that you are the same God of us all—a God of love." Throughout the year, the pastor continued to pray similar prayers.

Have you ever been in a situation in which someone told you, "Yes, Jesus may be true for you, but for someone else, they may believe something different"? I think my pastor was attempting to welcome students with a diverse range of spiritual beliefs. Some of the students of other faiths included my Muslim friends from Egypt, as well as my basketball teammate from Senegal. But I knew that Jesus had said, "I am the way, the truth, and the life. *No one comes to the Father, except through me"* (John 14:6; my italics). I also knew that the early historical church believed that "there is salvation in no one else, for there is no other name under heaven given to men by which we must be saved" (Acts 4:12). First-century Christians believed firmly that salvation was only through Jesus and faith in his death and resurrection.

What I experienced as a high school student wasn't unusual for many young Christians. In fact, today, if you claim that your religion is exclusively true, you are often regarded as an intolerant, narrow-minded, bigoted extremist. I started praying and a couple of weeks later, I approached the pastor. I mustered up the courage to ask if he would allow me to preach for him some Sunday morning in church. Before this, I didn't have a strong desire to speak or teach, but I became convinced that the student body needed to hear the truth and love of Jesus Christ. To my surprise the pastor said, "Yes!" I was nervous, but I knew I needed to start preparing.

As I was praying, I felt led by the Lord to talk to a particular student named Scott. I didn't know why God wanted me to go to Scott's room, but I thought that maybe God would use me to tell him about Jesus. So, I showed up at his dorm and introduced myself.

I said, "Scott, I know this seems weird, but I believe that God wants us to have a Bible study right now, even though we both have a lot of homework. I don't know how to lead a Bible study, but I am actually working on my first sermon and am a little nervous about public speaking, so I thought I could practice it for you. You could critique me, and then we could pray."

Scott said, "Go ahead; let's do it."

I asked Scott's roommate Ethan to join us, and even though it was a little awkward, I started preaching to the two of them. I gave a simple sermon, similar to evangelist Billy Graham's style, on John 3:16 (NKJV): "For God so loved the world, that he gave his only begotten Son, that whoever believes in him should not perish but have everlasting life." At the end of my message, I practiced giving an invitation for anyone in the audience who wanted to accept Christ.

When I was finished, Ethan said, "That's really good. When you give that message at church, I am going to pray to receive Christ."

I looked at him, a little astonished, and said, "You can pray to trust Jesus as your Savior right now." I said a prayer out loud, and he repeated it as he prayed to trust Jesus.

As we finished praying, a couple of guys walked by the room. They seemed surprised to see me there and asked what we were doing. I said, "Guys, we're having a Bible study. Come on in!" I gave the same message on John 3:16 to them, and when I was done, one of the guys said, "Dave, that makes sense. I need to believe in Jesus." Once again, I led this student in a simple prayer for him to trust in Christ. I told these guys to come back the next day and bring some friends. When I arrived the next day, there were several new people in the room, and as I practiced the same sermon, two more young men prayed to receive Christ. I announced to the group that we needed to start a weekly Bible study and asked them to bring some more friends the next week. That night, I set an important goal for myself: to personally tell every single student on that campus about Christ.

On one occasion, I was having a conversation with a friend of mine in the library who was an outspoken lesbian. I shared with her about the love of God through Christ. She began weeping when I started telling her how much God loved her. I was a little shocked at the sight of her tears, especially since I didn't think I said anything offensive. She then shared with me how much she was hurting on the inside and that she had become convicted of her sin and wanted to receive the love of Christ. The group grew, and people I didn't expect started coming. A couple of my Muslim friends showed up, one guy who claimed to be a Satanist dropped by, and others who were agnostics and atheists also attended.

We had a question-and-answer time after each session, and some people started to ask tough questions. They asked about the truth of the Bible, about other religions, about salvation by grace (as opposed to salvation by works), and about religious exclusivity.

These were hard questions, and I didn't have all of the answers. Weeks later, I preached at the church, and people responded positively to the good news of salvation through Jesus. Even the pastor was encouraging of my message.

Doors started opening for me to speak at other small churches in the area, and people also started asking more questions about Christianity. Again, I didn't know all of the answers. Even though it was exciting at times to see people become interested in Jesus, it wasn't always easy. In fact, sometimes it got downright discouraging, because some of the people who prayed to "trust Jesus" ended up walking away from Christianity and others stopped coming to Bible study. Some people started asking challenging questions, and I didn't know the answers. The spiritual "high" I had experienced seemed to be slipping away.

As I struggled with these disappointments, I was challenged to grow in my love for Christ while also learning how to defend my faith. After high school, I decided to attend Liberty University in Lynchburg, Virginia. I wanted to attend a Christian university where I could study the Bible and have Christian community. As I was studying the Bible, I threw myself into ministry, doing juvenile prison ministry, street evangelism, overseas mission trips, and leading youth camps. Students frequently asked me tough questions, and I knew I needed to give them answers. Whenever they asked a question I couldn't answer, I replied, "That's a great question. I'm not sure. But let me get back to you."

I graduated from Liberty a year early, moved to Dallas, and spent that year as a traveling intern with Christian apologist Josh McDowell to conferences across the United States, as well as Russia and Poland. At the universities in Poland, I listened to Josh's lectures on the historical reliability of the Bible. I noticed a strong influence of scientism, socialism, and relativism in the minds of my peers, not only at universities in the U.S. but around the world.

My passion was evangelism, but I realized that to be effective in evangelism, I needed to grow in apologetics. One day as Josh was speaking, I met another speaker, Dr. Norman Geisler. Geisler stood up without any notes and with humor told how he had been drawn into Christian apologetics. He talked about how as a young Christian, he was evangelizing on the streets of Detroit, when an intoxicated man staggered up to him and slurred, "I'm a graduate of Moody InstaBibletute and you shouldn't be doing this." Geisler asked him, "Doing what?" The man responded, "Evangelizing and telling people what to believe." The man then said, "Give me your Bible." And he opened it immediately to a passage in Matthew 8:4, "Jesus said to him, 'Go and tell no man.'" The young Geisler looked at his Bible and sure enough, that's what it said! The man said, "See? Now get out of here." Geisler knew that if Mormons, Jehovah's Witnesses, and even this stranger could trip him up with questions and objections, he had better start getting answers.

As I listened to Geisler's lecture, I was amazed at how he used the tools of logic against self-refuting statements when skeptics attack our faith. Geisler was like a walking encyclopedia, explaining how to refute objections to Christianity. After his lecture, he gave me his business card and told me that he had cofounded a seminary with the dual emphasis of apologetics and evangelism in Charlotte, North Carolina. He said, "Come visit my wife Barb and me, and I'll show you around Charlotte and you can earn a master's degree in apologetics." So, when my internship with Josh McDowell was complete, I moved to Charlotte. I was a youth pastor on weekends and sold furniture during the day; but for two evenings each week, for three years, I took apologetics courses from Dr. Norman Geisler, Dr. Barry Leventhal, and Dr. Thomas Howe.

My first year in seminary, I was the youngest student at age twenty-two and felt like I knew a lot less than the others. But I knew the Lord could use the knowledge I did have to share truth to high school and middle school students. I still encourage my friends today: "You may not be an expert in apologetics, but you can keep studying and share the knowledge that you do have with someone younger in the faith."

Dr. and Mrs. Geisler had the students over on occasional Saturday nights for "fireside chats" where we could ask tough questions about particular issues. I was often amazed how he answered with such clarity, both philosophically and biblically. Now, years later, I'm still seeking answers to some questions, but I'm also constantly learning how to better share my faith with others and give an adequate defense of the message of Jesus Christ.

At my church, we have a large recovery ministry on Monday nights called Regeneration that attracts people from all walks of life who have addictions, hurts, and hang-ups. For those who aren't sure if Christianity is even true, we invite them to come to a large room with comfortable couches where they can ask any questions. We call this ministry Great Questions and reassure seekers by letting them know that no question is off limits. I encourage churches to incorporate similar ministries to create inviting atmospheres for spiritual seekers and open-minded skeptics.

What Is Apologetics?

Apologetics is a term that simply means to give a defense or reason. There are some Christians who claim to "follow the Bible," but they're skeptical about argument, reasoning, and apologetics in evangelism. In response to this kind of attitude, I encourage my Christian friends to remember that Jesus himself said the greatest commandment was to "love the LORD your God with all your heart, all your soul, and *all your mind*" (Matt. 22:37 NLT; my italics).

Too many people mistakenly believe that the Christian faith is a "blind faith" to a "leap of faith." Jesus, however, doesn't ask us to make a leap of blind faith in the dark, but rather to take a step of faith in the light—the light of evidence. This doesn't mean that God reveals all our answers to life immediately. Jesus called his disciples first and then spent three years with them, living out a life they could observe and trust. They still had a lot of questions after his physical resurrection! However, the trust to which God calls us is not opposed to reason. My mentor, Dr. Geisler, told me, "We should heed the Socratic dictum that the unexamined life is not worth living by insisting that the unexamined faith is not worth believing."

More than four hundred years before Jesus was born in Bethlehem, the great Greek philosopher Socrates was put on trial and charged with corrupting the minds of the youth of Athens and impiety for not believing in the gods of the state. He stood and gave his defense, which was called *The Apology (Apologia)* and recorded by his student, Plato. The Greek word *apologia* means to give a verbal defense or a reasoned statement or argument. Since the New Testament was written in the Greek language, this same Greek word was used multiple times, which is where we get the word *apologetics*, which for us means to make a case or defend the faith. It is most frequently translated as "defense." The early evangelists of Christianity provided reasoned defenses of Christianity and were frequently called "apologists."

Let's look at the uses of this word in the New Testament. First, we see Paul using it in a legal sense similar to Socrates when he is being falsely accused and his critics are trying to sentence him to death:

> "Brothers and fathers, hear the *defense* [*apologia*] that I now make before you." (Acts 22:1 ESV; my italics)

Paul is later falsely charged by some chief priests who partnered with the Roman leaders to sentence him to death. Yet Paul, knowing his legal rights as a Roman citizen, said,

> "I answered them that it is not the custom of the Romans to hand over any man before the accused meets his accusers face to face and has an opportunity to make his *defense* [*apologia*] against the charges." (Acts 25:16 ESV)

Paul used this same word when writing to the church of Philippi to describe how he is both proclaiming and defending the gospel:

Both in my imprisonment and in *the defense* [*apologia*] and confirmation of the gospel, you all are partakers of grace with me. (Phil. 1:7 ESV)

Apologetics was important to Paul, as we see here in his letter to the Philippians:

I am appointed for the *defense* [*apologia*] of the gospel.
(Phil. 1:16 ESV)

Peter also uses this word and encourages believers to be ready:

Always being prepared to make *a defense* [*apologia*] to anyone who asks you for a reason for the hope that is in you; yet do it with gentleness and respect. (1 Pet. 3:15 ESV)

One major insight about apologetics gained from Scripture is that it is both offensive and defensive. Championships aren't won by just playing defense; you have to also score. When I'm teaching young people the game of basketball, I remind them that if you don't get buckets, you don't win. Some people assume that apologetics is just giving a "defense" and answering tough questions. That's part of it! But apologetics can also be going on the *offense*. As Christians, we can go on the *offense* without being offensive. After we have listened, we can be a Christian case maker and provide some reasons why the best explanation for the cause of the universe, the existence of laws of nature, and objective moral standards is God.

It's so important to set the conversation up through questions and create a spark of interest before making the positive case for Christianity. Apple founder Steve Jobs followed an innovative principle from Henry Ford that can be applied to the way we initiate conversation as Christ followers:

I think Henry Ford once said, "If I'd asked customers what they wanted, they would have told me, 'A faster horse!'" People don't know what they want until you show it to them. That's why I never rely on market research. Our task is to read things that are not yet on the page.[1]

In evangelism, you may be talking to an atheist or apathetic agnostic who isn't interested in arguments for the gospel of Jesus, God's existence, or the truthfulness of the "Romans Road." But you can go on offense and ask some questions that might stir some curiosity, and then they may become more interested in seeing why arguments for God's existence—without using the Bible—are important.

I've said the following in my conversations with nonbelievers:

- Both you as an atheist and me as a Christian believe in the laws of nature. How do you account for their existence?

- Both you as an atheist and me as a theist believe that some acts (like enslaving people based on the color of their skin) are objectively wrong. We both know this is wrong, so where do moral laws come from?

- Can you explain to me what caused the big bang?

- On a scale from 1 to 10, how certain are you that God does not exist?

After stumbling for a response, many say to me, "Well, you explain to me your answer." Then I'm able to give arguments for God's existence without opening a Bible. In the next chapter, we will examine some specific reasons for God's existence—even without using the Bible.

9

REASONS FOR GOD'S EXISTENCE WITHOUT THE BIBLE

There are a couple of dozen logical arguments for God's existence, and it's important for all Christians to become familiar with at least some of them. If God does not exist, then the spiritual seeker will not believe that the Bible is the word of God. If an atheist does not believe that God exists, then it won't make sense to believe that Jesus is God. If an atheist or agnostic is skeptical about God's existence, then they'll likely be skeptical of miracles, which are described in the Bible as supernatural acts by God.

By using the acronym G-O-D, I'd like to share with you three basic arguments you can use to quickly explain to an unbeliever some reasons for God's existence. This tool is also helpful for training Christians in memorizing these for confidence and clarity. These arguments provide the best explanation for the following:

- **G** The standard of all GOOD in the universe
- **O** The powerful ORIGIN of the universe
- **D** The grand DESIGN of the universe

One of the objections toward arguments of God's existence from agnostics and atheists is that they are simply "God-of-the-gaps-fallacies." The God-of the-gaps fallacy is the position that assumes an act of God as the reason for some unknown phenomenon. The famous atheist Friedrich Nietzsche said, "Into every gap they [priests] put their delusion, their stopgap, which they call God."[1] The atheist will argue that Christians are merely making an argument from ignorance, saying something like: "They can't explain the beginning of the universe, so they assume God did it. They can't explain unusual occurrences on which science hasn't reached a consensus, so they assume God did it." But let's be clear that what we're talking about is not an argument from ignorance but a *positive case* using deductive arguments for which if the premises are true, then the conclusion *necessarily follows.*

"G" Reason #1: There Is a Standard of *Good* in the Universe (The Moral Argument)

God is the best explanation for a standard of good in the universe, which some call the moral argument for God's existence. The moral argument can be stated in this logical progression:

1. If God does not exist, then objective moral values and duties do not exist.

2. Objective moral values and duties do exist.

3. Therefore, God exists.

If God does not exist, then why is anything really good or really bad? And, if God does not exist, why does anything exist at all? But even if a purely material or physical universe existed apart from a Supreme Being, why would there be a standard of right and wrong that was objective for all people in all times and cultures? You and I can't go into a scientific laboratory and see "goodness" or "badness." If God does not exist, then aren't we just the result of a blind evolutionary process of change? Atheist Richard Dawkins said,

> The universe that we observe has precisely the properties we should expect if there is, at bottom, no design, no purpose, no evil, no good, nothing but pitiless indifference.[2]

If we're nothing but molecules, then we can't prove that Nazi doctor Joseph Mengele, who performed deadly human experiments at Auschwitz, was morally wrong to do so. To say that these acts are wrong is to assume there is a moral absolute. William Lane Craig writes,

> On the atheistic view, human beings are just animals, and animals have no moral obligations to one another. When a lion kills a zebra, it kills the zebra, but it does not murder the zebra. When a great white shark forcibly copulates with a female, it forcibly copulates with her but it does not rape her—for there is not moral dimension to these actions. They are neither prohibited nor obligatory.[3]

Premise #1: If God does not exist, then objective moral values and duties do not exist.

Some atheists will object to premise #1. They will say, "There are a lot of atheists who live good moral lives and they don't believe in God." But the argument isn't saying that atheists can't live good moral lives. Nor does the argument require that one must believe in God to believe in objective moral values and duties. Belief in God isn't necessary for an objective standard of goodness, but God's existence is necessary. Objective moral values and duties can exist only if a Moral Lawgiver (that is, God) exists.

Premise # 2: Objective moral values and duties do exist.

Let's look at premise #2. It's undeniable that our consciences have recognized an objective moral law. Throughout history, humans have understood that certain actions are objectively morally wrong and that other behaviors are objectively morally right. Many societies understand that we should "tell the truth," "not end human life," and "do unto others as you would want them to do unto you."

Some atheists will try to embrace moral relativism. Unfortunately, there have always been moral relativists, like the Greek philosopher Protagoras, who have attempted to teach that human beings are the ones who decide the moral standard. Protagoras said, "Man [humankind] is the measure of all things." People like Protagoras—who say there is no objective moral law (that is, the law of human nature or rule of decent behavior)—will say that if there is any moral law at all, then it is subjective or relative to the individual or culture. They will say, "You have your morals, I have mine," and "You shouldn't impose your moral beliefs on me." Others will take the words of Christ out of context and say, "Do not judge, or you will be judged." But notice how this statement appeals to a "should not" or "do not." By their own admission, even moral relativists appeal to a transcendent standard of how one should or should not behave.

Another difficulty with this relativistic thinking is that it leaves the question, "Which person is the measure of things?" Therefore, I would ask a moral relativist: What human being determines the standard? Is it the single mother who sacrificially provides for her three children, or is it the unfaithful, lazy guy who left her for another woman? Who is our ultimate standard? Is it Mother Teresa? Adolf Hitler? Donald J. Trump? Barack Obama? Billy Graham?

Even though people disagree about certain aspects of the law of human nature, humankind has historically recognized the law. C. S. Lewis wrote:

> Men have differed as regards what people you ought to be unselfish to—whether it was only your own family, or your fellow countrymen, or everyone. But they have always agreed that you ought not to put yourself first. Selfishness has never been admired. Men have differed as to whether you should have one wife or four. But they have always agreed that you must not simply have any woman you liked. . . . But the most remarkable thing is this. Whenever you find a man who says he does not believe in a real Right and Wrong, you will find the same man going back on this a moment later.[4]

Another way of stating a moral argument is:

1. Every law has a lawgiver.

2. There is a moral law.

3. Therefore, there is a moral lawgiver.

Let's make some observations about this conclusion. After briefly stating this argument, you might ask, "Don't you agree that the giver of this law is not you and it's not me?" We recognize that throughout history certain societies have behaved badly, so we observe that the giver of the moral law cannot be a particular society either. The giver of this law must be something or someone transcendent, something or someone beyond us. Dr. Martin Luther King, Jr. said it this way:

> But I'm here to say to you this morning that some things are right and some things are wrong. Eternally so, absolutely so. It's wrong to hate. It always has been wrong and it always will be wrong. It's wrong in America, it's wrong in Germany, it's wrong in Russia, it's wrong in China. It was wrong in 2000 B.C., and it's wrong in 1954 A.D. It always has been wrong, (That's right!) and it always will be wrong. (That's right!) It's wrong to throw our lives away in riotous living. No matter if everybody in Detroit is doing it, it's wrong. It always will be wrong, and it always has been wrong. It's wrong in every age and it's wrong in every nation. Some things are right and some things are wrong, no matter if everybody is doing the contrary. Some things in this universe are absolute. The God of the universe has made it so. And so long as we adopt this relative attitude toward right and wrong, we're revolting against the very laws of God himself. [5]

Premise #3: Therefore, God exists.

King strongly believed that an absolute moral law exists and therefore that a moral lawgiver must exist. The moral lawgiver is transcendent and supreme to the universe and time. So, we can we say that God is "G," the best explanation for an objective standard of goodness. Although these reasons don't necessarily demand that this being is the Triune God of Christianity, it's certainly consistent with the theistic God of Scripture.

"O" Reason #2: God Is the Best Explanation for the *Origin* or Beginning of the Universe (The Cosmological Argument)

This argument is also known as the cosmological argument. This line of reasoning asserts that there is a First Cause of the cosmos (or universe). Simply put, the argument develops like this:

1. Everything that had a beginning had a cause.

2. The universe had a beginning.

3. Therefore, the universe had a cause.

Premise #1: Everything that had a beginning had a cause.

In science class, we learned the principle of causality that says everything that begins needs a cause. Without this principle, science would be impossible. Even the great skeptic David Hume couldn't deny the law of causality. "I never asserted so absurd a proposition," he wrote, "as that something could arise without a cause."[6] If someone ever tells you that the Law of Causality is not real, ask them, "What *caused* you to come to that conclusion?"

Premise #2: The universe had a beginning.

The second premise says that the universe had a beginning. Although this may seem obvious now, at the start of the twentieth century, quite a few scientists believed the universe was eternal with no beginning. In the last century, however, an abundance of scientific discoveries has affirmed that the universe must have had a beginning. In 1927, the influential cosmologist Edwin Hubble observed through his telescope, by means of the movements of distant galaxies and the wavelengths of their light, that the universe was expanding. Hubble's discovery has caused most astronomers to conclude that the universe had an absolute beginning, because they understand that if we were to hypothetically reverse the expansion, we would arrive at nothing—the point at which the expansion began. As physicist Stephen Hawking puts it, "Almost everyone now believes that the universe, and *time itself*, had a beginning at the Big Bang."[7]

Many scientists even identify the big bang with God's acts of creation as recorded in Genesis. Scientist Gerald Schroeder, who earned his PhD in physics from MIT, says,

> Creation, in biblical language, refers to the Eternal's introduction into the universe of something from nothing. It is an instantaneous act. Genesis 1:1 is teaching that in the beginning, in an instantaneous flash now known as the Big Bang, God created from absolute nothing the raw materials of the universe.

Similarly, agnostic astrophysicist Robert Jastrow wrote,

> Now we see how the astronomical evidence leads to a biblical view of the origin of the world. The details differ, but the essential elements and the astronomical and biblical accounts of Genesis are the same; the chain of events leading to man commenced suddenly and sharply at a definite moment in time, in a flash of light and energy.[8]

Premise #3: Therefore, the universe had a cause.

If it's true that the universe had a definite beginning, then it takes only a small step of faith into the light to believe that *someone* caused the universe to exist. But it takes a huge step of faith into the dark to believe that *no one* caused the universe to exist. If someone did create the universe, then that being must have been powerful. If matter came into existence, then the cause would have to be immaterial. The cause would most likely be something personal, like an immaterial mind. And if time came into existence, then the cause would have to be timeless or eternal. Although this argument doesn't tell us anything about this cause's attributes, it does suggest characteristics to the being whom philosophers and theologians refer to as *God*.

"D" Reason 3: God Is the Best Explanation for the Design or Fine-Tuning of the Universe (Intelligent Design Theory)

This argument says that God is the best explanation of the design, or fine-tuning, of the universe. The design may be observed in several areas, such as the intricate astronomical evidence of the universe's origin or the detailed information discovered in DNA. Most proponents of Intelligent Design (ID) believe it's more probable that the universe was designed purposely by some form of intelligence than by pure chance or luck. Although proponents of ID don't necessarily believe the universe was designed by God, it's true that many of them will acknowledge that only a being who is powerful (like God) could design the universe. Even the famous atheist Richard Dawkins, who claims to be antagonistic toward the concept of an Intelligent Designer, in his interview with Ben Stein hinted at the possibility that *aliens* could have designed the world.

Modern atheists will use arguments similar to the ancient philosopher Lucretius, who appealed to the imperfections of the world to disprove that God was the creator. But imperfect design still implies a designer. When atheists ask why an all-benevolent being would create a world with natural disasters, disease, and death, they are actually asking a theological question about the nature of God. The design argument doesn't defend the character of God's goodness or perfection. ID simply argues that empirical evidence in the universe suggests the existence of a designer.

Let me share another analogy. Suppose you visited the Louvre Museum in Paris and found yourself gazing at one of the world's most popular paintings, the *Mona Lisa*. Would you conclude that this was just an accident from an explosion in a paint store? You're more likely to assume that this remarkable work was done by an accomplished painter (designer).

The argument from design was popularized by an Anglican theologian, William Paley, who published *Natural Theology* in 1837. Paley wrote,

> In crossing a heath, supposed I pitched my foot against a *stone*, and were asked how the stone came to be there, I might possibly answer, for anything I knew to the contrary, it had lain there forever. But suppose I found a *watch* upon the ground; I should hardly think of the answer I had given before.[9]

Paley was making the point that you don't have to be an expert in watches or even stones to understand that someone designed the watch. While you may not know who exactly created the watch, you know someone did.

Some Darwinian naturalistic atheists will criticize this argument by showing its limitations in describing the nature of the Intelligent Designer. These same atheists often fail to admit that faith is also involved in some of the mysteries of evolution. Just as there are some things we don't understand about Intelligent Design, naturalistic scientists do not fully understand evolution. Once again, Intelligent Design doesn't attempt to describe all of the moral attributes of God (love, justice, mercy, etc.). It simply claims that it's more likely that the probability of fine-tuning points toward intelligence rather than accident or happenstance.

Astronomer Hugh Ross has identified hundreds of examples that suggest the universe was precisely created and "tweaked" to support human life on earth. For example, the size of our galaxy is perfect. If the Milky Way was larger, infusions of gas and stars would disturb the sun's orbit and cause too many galactic eruptions. If it was smaller, then there would be an insufficient infusion of gas to sustain star formation. Similarly, the oxygen and nitrogen quantities are just right for life. If there was more oxygen, then plants and hydrocarbons would burn up too easily. If there was less oxygen, then advanced animals would have too little to breathe. Given these and hundreds of other examples of precise "fine-tuning" in the universe, it is *most* probable, beyond a reasonable doubt, that an Intelligent Designer was involved in the creation of the universe.

While writing this book, I took a full-time job as an account executive with Foundation Medicine, an innovative biotechnology company known as comprehensive genomic profiling, testing a large panel of three hundred genes across four main classes of genomic alterations. Cancer is often caused by abnormal cell growth caused by DNA or RNA mutations. This testing can discover unique genetic mutations that cause cancer, and the company partners with pharmaceutical companies that are coming up with precise treatments to particular mutations.

During my initial two-week training at their headquarters in Cambridge, Massachusetts, I learned a lot about cancer and precision medicine; but for a couple of days, I felt like I was relearning the basics of biology I should have remembered from high school and college. When learning the basics of cell biology, I was reminded of how complicated and yet how *finely tuned* the human cell is and the implications of coding, language, and replication that take place within the cell.

I'll summarize what can be watched in the "From DNA to Protein" short video referenced below.[10] You may recall from high school biology that the nucleus of the cell contains the genome. In humans, the genome is split between 23 pairs of chromosomes. Each chromosome contains a long strand of DNA. Within the DNA are sections called genes. These genes have the instructions for making proteins. DNA has four chemical groups called bases: adenine, guanine, cytosine, and thymine. When looking at these bases, even the most adamant naturalist recognizes that they function like a language. An enzyme known as RNA polymerase attaches to the gene and moves along the DNA, making a strand of messenger RNA. The DNA codes determine the order in which the bases are added to the RNA. This process is called *transcription*.

In my company training, I was reminded of the basics of cell biology so I could eventually learn about mutations and be able to have conversations with oncologists concerning their cancer patients. In addition to relearning cell basics, I was also reminded of how finely tuned the human genome is. The structure and order of a person's DNA also support the theory of Intelligent Design.

Dr. Francis Collins is one of the leading DNA scientists in the world and head of the Human Genome Project. In his book *The Language of God*, he reveals that he is a man of unshakable faith in God and Scripture. Collins recalls an announcement about the Human Genome Project in the year 2000 that appeared in virtually every major newspaper. He stood with President Bill Clinton and was joined by Prime Minister Tony Blair by satellite. In his address, President Clinton said,

> Without a doubt, this is the most important, most wondrous map ever produced by humankind. Today, we are learning the language in which God created life. We are gaining ever more awe for the complexity, the beauty, and the wonder of God's most divine and sacred gift.

Reflecting on Clinton's speech, Collins noted,

> The part of his speech that most attracted public attention jumped from the scientific perspective to the spiritual. Was I, a rigorously trained scientist, taken aback at such a blatantly religious reference by the leader of the free world at a moment like this? No, not at all.[11]

Francis Collins is one of many scientists who don't see a problem in believing that science points to God.

Now a critic will look at mutations that cause illness and ask, "How could this be designed with such imperfections like cancer?"

But this is a theological question, questioning whether the designer is morally good or perfect. Imperfect design still implies design. In providing an argument, we're making the case that a designer is the best explanation of the design. You don't have to give an explanation of the explanation.

Later on, you may want to talk about how sin came into the world and that the whole universe is groaning and cursed, as Romans 8 describes, but you don't have to go there at this point in your conversation. You also don't have to be an expert in science or philosophy to see that evidence of the design in the universe implies, beyond a reasonable doubt, an Intelligent Designer. For many years, Antony Flew was known as one of the world's leading atheists. But Flew abandoned his atheism and accepted the existence of God because of the argument from design. In an interview for *Philosophia Christi* with Gary Habermas, Flew explained his new beliefs: "I had to go where the evidence leads."[12]

When we evangelize, these three arguments may not necessarily convert a skeptic to Christ immediately. However, you can encourage them *to go where the evidence leads*. Perhaps these three arguments will help someone leave their atheism and believe that there must be something or someone out there. Sometimes I wonder how atheists such as Richard Dawkins can admit that aliens might have been involved in the creation of our world but get angry when someone suggests that the world's designer is God. Perhaps it's because if God exists, then there are moral implications for the way we live our lives and treat one another.

This may be a reminder that sometimes it's a heart issue and not purely an intellectual objection. We should, then, address both the intellect and the heart and give evidence of God's goodness and design. Although there are many reasons to show that God exists, we can start by demonstrating that God is the best explanation for a standard of "G" goodness, "O" the origin of the universe, and the "D" design in the universe.

10

ENGAGING OTHER RELIGIONS

A while back, I was speaking at a conference in North Carolina, where one of my former professors from Liberty University, Dr. Gary Habermas, was one of the keynote speakers. Dr. Habermas introduced me to Dr. Nabeel Qureshi, a young medical doctor who was attending the conference. Dr. Habermas, who is one of the leading scholars on the resurrection of Jesus, told me how he met Nabeel when Nabeel was a Muslim and skeptical of the resurrection. As I mentioned earlier, Muslims don't believe that Jesus historically died. Nabeel began sharing with me his story and his conversion from Islam to believing that Jesus did die and also rose again from the dead. I was amazed by his passion and commitment to truth. As he was sharing with me, other speakers gathered around to listen to why he became a Christian.

When Nabeel was a Muslim, he studied Islamic apologetics and often engaged Christians in religious discussions, although they rarely could defend what they believed. But one friend, David Wood, was different. David defended his beliefs historically and philosophically, and he challenged Nabeel on some of his assumptions. Through a long journey and many conversations, Nabeel was drawn to the person of Jesus. He tells the story in his fascinating book, *Seeking Allah, Finding Jesus*.[1]

A couple years later, a well-known apologist invited twenty other apologists to spend a few days with his staff at their organization to talk about apologetics, culture, and evangelism. Nabeel had just joined this staff as a full-time apologist. Over those few days, I asked Nabeel many questions about Islam, Mohammed, and the Qur'an. Ever since I was a senior in high school, I've had a desire to become more effective in witnessing to Muslims, but I wanted to gain wisdom from those who left Islam to become Christians.

Nabeel was an excellent communicator. He loved Jesus and he loved people. On one occasion, while we were in Colorado at a Christian camp, about a hundred high school students gathered around the porch and asked Nabeel questions for several hours. His ministry grew rapidly, and he was soon speaking at Ivy League universities and large conferences. Then, in his early thirties, Nabeel developed stomach cancer and within a short time went to be with the Lord, leaving behind his wife and young daughter. Some Muslims on the Internet trolled him and said, "The reason you're getting cancer is because you became a Christian. Allah is judging you."

Before he died, Nabeel said, "Death is nothing to be feared. Jesus has conquered it, and we are in him. His resurrection has been the focus of Christian confidence from the inception of the church." Nabeel, like a growing number of Muslims, realized that the Qur'an had incorrectly taught about the very person of Jesus. He was changed both intellectually and relationally by the power of Christ.

In this chapter, I'd like to give a brief overview of some of the more popular world religions, and then I'll guide you with a few good questions to consider asking. As you read, keep in mind these four important points:

1. You don't have to be an expert in other religions: learn as you go!

2. Observe how other religions redefine Jesus.

3. Be patient with the process and consider building friendships.

4. Pray for the Holy Spirit to work supernaturally.

You Don't Have to Be an Expert in Other Religions: Learn as You Go!

Let me share several words of overview and encouragement. You don't have to be an expert in all the religions before you can be useful in your Jesus Conversations. If you're talking to your Muslim coworker, Hindu neighbor, or if perhaps a Jehovah's Witness or Mormon shows up to your door, have a conversation with them!

We can simply start the conversation. I learn a lot by asking a few basic questions. Listen and use the tools of logic, and then tell them the gospel truth. As you ask questions, you may find them contradicting their own beliefs. Keep calm and confident in the Lord. Don't assume that every Muslim or Mormon you meet believes everything you've studied about that particular religion. They may not even know it! (Just like many professing American "Christians" know little about genuine faith!)

It's good for us to have an understanding and grow in understanding of popular religions so we can ask followers the right questions. I heard an evangelist tell a story about a time she met a man whose job was to examine hundred-dollar bills and find the counterfeit ones. She asked him, "I bet you have to spend a lot of time studying the counterfeit in order to recognize them." He responded, "No, I invest my time studying the real thing so I know what is not real." In the same way, as Christians we must spend more time studying and learning theology about the true and living God of the Bible so we can recognize what is not true. Don't get discouraged if you don't know certain details about other religions; you'll learn as you go.

Observe How Other Religions Redefine Jesus

Many false religions will add Jesus to their other beliefs. Some will say, "We believe in Jesus, plus we believe in other revelations, gods, and prophets." Or they'll subtract from Jesus and say, "Jesus was a very good man, but not God." The apostle Paul warned the church about someone coming to them and preaching "a Jesus other than the Jesus we preached" (2 Cor. 11:4). He cautioned the church of Galatia about "a different gospel which is really no gospel at all" and that some people were "trying to pervert the gospel of Christ" (Gal. 1:7). Paul strongly admonished them:

> But even if we or an angel from heaven should preach a gospel other than the one we preached to you, let him be eternally condemned! As we have already said, so now I say again: If anyone is preaching to you a gospel other than what you accepted, let him be eternally condemned! (Gal. 1:8)

Notice Paul's boldness. He was firm in his conviction and strongly rebuked anyone who would try to redefine Jesus or the gospel.

My dad ministered in India several times. He found that Hindus might respond to the message about Jesus in a positive way and then go home and put a picture of Jesus in their living room alongside many other Hindu idols! Therefore, preachers in India must clarify the uniqueness of Jesus and that Jesus must be the *only* way to God (John 14:6).

Be Patient with the Process and Consider Building Friendships

When we share the good news with those of other faiths, we should remember that the process and decision might take longer than explaining the gospel to a nominal Catholic or backslidden Baptist who already affirms the deity of Jesus and has a high view of the Bible. The gospel in itself is simple, but persuading someone to give up pantheism (the belief that "all is God") to believe in theism ("God made all") often takes a while. The same could be said for transforming a person's mind who doesn't believe that Jesus is divine to believing in his deity.

Acts 17:17 says that Paul "reasoned in the synagogue with the Jews and the God-fearing Greeks, as well as in the marketplace *day by day* with those who happened to be there" (my italics). With people who believe in other religions, the process frequently takes longer. We can learn from the example of the apostles, who at times reasoned for long periods to evangelize and teach. In Acts 14, Luke writes that in Iconium, "Paul and Barnabas spent *considerable time* there, speaking boldly for the Lord" (my italics). Campus ministries that spend time getting to know international students and serving them can make a powerful impact, but it may not be a quick conversion overnight because of close family ties to another religion that is ingrained in their culture. Another thing I have done is invite Muslims to meet for a few weeks to read the Gospels, which may allow an opportunity for the Holy Spirit to enlighten their hearts and minds with the good news of Jesus.

Pray for the Holy Spirit to Work Supernaturally

In dealing with other religions, we must pray that God will intervene to do the supernatural. God can still use supernatural revelation—perhaps a dream, a vision, or a special messenger—in reaching the hearts of unbelievers. Nabeel Qureshi experienced several visions when he was a Muslim considering Christianity. Many leading evangelical theologians believe that God works this way to get a person of another religion to focus on Jesus. Dr. Norman Geisler explained,

> While it is normative (and perhaps more fruitful) for God to use believers to bring the gospel to the unevangelized, it is possible that He may use other means at His disposal to deliver the message of the gospel to those who would never believe it. One day God will use an angel to preach the gospel "to every nation, tribe, language and people [Rev. 14:6]. Historically, God

has miraculously conveyed special revelation through visions and dreams. God is more willing that all be saved than we are [2 Pet. 3:9].[2]

A well-known apologist once said to Lee Strobel,

> I have spoken in many Islamic countries, where it's tough to talk about Jesus. Virtually every Muslim who has come to follow Christ has done so, first, because the love of Christ expressed through a Christian, or second, because of a vision, a dream, or some other supernatural intervention. Now, no religion has a more intricate doctrine of angels and visions than Islam, and I think it's extraordinary that God uses that sensitivity to the supernatural world in which he speaks in visions and dreams and reveals himself. One of India's greatest converts was a Sikh, Sundar Singh, who came to know Christ through an appearance of Christ in his room in a dream one night. It had a tremendous impact on his life and he became a Christian. So there are ways that God can reveal himself that go far beyond our own understanding.[3]

Although we can't examine all the various religions in this book, let's look at four specific religions Christians might encounter and suggest some good questions for each of them.

Judaism

Judaism has its roots in the Torah (the first five books of the Christian Bible), which is part of the *Tanakh* or the Hebrew Bible. Christians call this the "Old Testament." There are about fifteen million Jewish adherents to Judaism worldwide. It is the tenth largest religion, and extremely important for Christians. Like Judaism, Christians believe in one God who revealed himself to Adam, Abraham, Moses, and David. But distinctly, we believe that Jesus is the

Jewish Messiah (Yeshua). As Christians, we are optimistic based on the Scriptures that one day the Jewish people will look on him whom they've pierced and will be saved.

Christians also recognize that there have been innumerable anti-Semitic atrocities committed over the past two thousand years, and even still today. In the historical past, both Protestant and Catholic leaders have said and done evil things to the Jewish people. Jews have faced persecution throughout history, including the Holocaust, which took the lives of six million innocent Jews by Hitler's Nazi regime.

Although there are different sects within Judaism, there is that core belief in one God, the Torah, and the hope of a Messiah in the line of King David. As you may recall from reading the New Testament, there were disagreements even then among various Jewish factions about the Mosaic law, Scripture, angels, and the resurrection of the dead. Judaism is a monotheistic religion (like Islam and Christianity) that believes there is one God who created the universe out of nothing. But when evangelizing to a Jewish person today, don't assume what they believe. I've made this mistake several times. There are different sects and traditions that have changed substantially since the time of Abraham and Moses, and many American Jews are quite liberal in their thinking with no religious connections.

A couple of years ago, I was invited to go to Israel with Israel Collective[4] and a group of Christian leaders. On Friday night after visiting the Wailing Wall (or Western Wall), we went to a Jewish home to experience a Shabbat dinner with a Jewish family. As the host was leading us in some blessings in unison, which is part of the Shabbat meal, the host asked us to repeat a prayer that seemed to have some mystical phrases that included praying to spirits and reincarnation. Now this is certainly contrary to what we would think of as Orthodox Judaism, so I interrupted him and said, "Our group really appreciates you having us in your home for this lovely dinner, but we cannot repeat these things after you and do not feel comfortable hearing them, because we pray to God, the Father, and his Son Jesus Christ." It was an awkward moment and several people in my group joked for the rest of the evening about me going evangelistic and interrupting the Shabbat dinner. It certainly was an awkward dinner afterwards, but I learned not to assume that just because a person is Jewish, they have the same strong theistic traditions contained in the writings of the Old Testament. I also felt like I wasn't too persuasive as I spoke up. The next morning, Dr. William Lane Craig, who is one of Christianity's top defenders of the faith, called out to me as I was walking down the street: "David, I want you to know that what you did last night was courageous. You had a very legitimate concern about what this man was saying, and I am glad you spoke up." His words greatly encouraged me, especially coming from such a seasoned theologian and debater. Through that experience, I was reminded of several lessons. First, don't assume what a person of a particular religion believes. And second, be willing to speak up if someone says anything contrary to the gospel.

I've had interesting conversations with Jewish people of faith who practiced Judaism. When I was living in north Dallas, I often wrote and graded papers at a Starbucks near a couple of synagogues. I met with one rabbi who tutored students in Hebrew. I asked him questions about the suffering passage in Isaiah 53, such as, "Who is the one who was pierced for our transgressions, crushed for our iniquities"? He told me it was the Jewish people. I asked other questions about passages but seemed to go nowhere.

Around that time, I frequented a local grocery store and often talked to the checker, a Jewish teenager with a Kippah on his head. One occasion, I stopped by the grocery store late at night when there were few others in the store. I read him a portion of Isaiah 53 without telling him the reference and asked him, "Who do you think that is a description of?" He replied, "Jesus?" After taking a couple minutes to explain the gospel, I encouraged him to place his faith in Christ. Several things we might want to ask our Jewish friends include:

- Who is this "one" in Isaiah 53 who was pierced for our transgressions and crushed for our iniquities?

- If it's true that Jesus died historically and rose again, would you be willing to trust that he is the Messiah?

- How much of the New Testament have you read?

- Who do you think Jesus is from a historical standpoint?

- How do you explain the early reporting, the empty tomb, and the eyewitness testimonies?

Islam

Islam is growing rapidly in America and will one day likely surpass Christianity in numbers. For example, in my city of Dallas, there were seventeen mosques in 2011 and in 2020 there were eighty-four. By the time you're reading this, there will likely be over a hundred. Muhammad, born in Mecca in AD 570 and died in 632, founded the religion of Islam more than five hundred years after Jesus' death and resurrection. Muslims believe Muhammad was the Prophet who proclaimed that there was only one God, which was previously taught by Adam, Abraham, Moses, and Jesus. When he was about forty years old, Muhammad said he was visited by Jibril (Gabriel) and received his first revelation from God. Around 610, he began proclaiming the Five Pillars of Islam. Through his military conquest, he gathered his converts from the Meccan tribes, as many of them had experienced hostility from Meccan polytheists. After traveling to Medina, he continued to build his following through his military leadership. In 629, he and his 10,000 Muslim converts marched into the city of Mecca. For his new religion, there was no separation between church and state. He sought to spread his Sharia law, but only through forceful submission to his prophetic status and Allah. Muhammed claimed he would receive "Ayah" (signs from God). Though he didn't read or write, his followers wrote down his sayings after his death, which formed the Qur'an. Muslims believed his sayings were the verbatim word of God, without any error. Though Muslims believe that only the Qur'an is the word of God, they have a high view of Muhammad's teaching and practices that were recorded in the Hadith and Sira.

When I've talked to former Muslims, I discovered that they rejected Islam because they had major concerns from a historical standpoint. Nabeel, when he was searching for the truth, explained how his friend David Wood showed in the very writings of Islam's earliest sources the following:

> [There were] additional traditions that challenged the idea of Muhammad's prophethood, each progressively more offensive. Muhammad had been poisoned; on his deathbed, he felt as if the poison were killing him; he had black magic cast on him; he revealed verses he later admitted had been from Satan; he tortured people for money; he led an attack on unarmed Jews; he caused his adopted son to divorce so he could marry his daughter-in-law Zainab; he told people to drink camel's urine. The list went on and on.[5]

Muhammad claimed that he had received revelation that Jesus did not actually die. He was adamant that Jesus was only a prophet and that he did not die. This, of course, is contrary to the core of Christian doctrine. All four Gospel accounts record that Jesus died historically. For example, Mark writes,

> With a loud cry, Jesus breathed his last. The curtain of the temple was torn in two from top to bottom. And when the centurion, who stood there in front of Jesus, saw how he died, he said, "Surely this man was the Son of God!" Some women were watching from a distance. Among them were Mary Magdalene, Mary the mother of James the younger and of Joseph, and Salome. In Galilee these women had followed him and cared for his needs. Many other women who had come up with him to Jerusalem were also there. (Mark 15:37–41)

Muslims adamantly reject this. This is what the Qur'an says:

> That they said (in boast), "We killed Christ Jesus the son of Mary, the Messenger of Allah"; but they killed him not, nor crucified him, but so it was made to appear to them, and those who differ therein are full of doubts, with no (certain) knowledge, but only conjecture to follow, for of a surety they killed him not: Nay, Allah raised him up unto Himself; and Allah is Exalted in Power, Wise.[6]

Here are some questions to ask a Muslim:

- If Jesus did not die, who made it appear that he did? Was it Allah?

- If Allah caused this deception, wouldn't he be responsible for people believing Jesus died, and therefore responsible for the start of Christianity? If Allah did not cause it, then how could he allow such deception to take place regarding one of his holy prophets?

- From a historical standpoint, why should I believe this one source by Muhammad in the seventh century, rather than multiple eyewitness sources in the first century?

- I understand you believe the Bible was corrupted. When exactly was it corrupted, and what is your historical evidence?

- If you became convinced historically that Jesus really did die and came back from the dead, would you be willing to become a Christian?

Mormonism

The Mormon religion (the Church of Jesus Christ of Latter-Day Saints) tries to appear as a mainstream Christian group and their advertisements promote wholesome family life. Joseph Smith, seen by his followers as a modern-day prophet, claimed in the 1820s that an angel led him to some "gold plates" in western New York, which he supposedly translated "by the gift and power of God" into the Book of Mormon. Smith told his followers that he had seen a vision of God in the spring of 1820 and was told that existing Christian churches "were all wrong . . . and their teachers were all corrupt." By 1830, Smith reported that he had been instructed that God would use him to reestablish the true Christian church and the Book of Mormon would be the means of establishing correct doctrine for the restored church.

However, not only does the Mormon church deny essential Christian doctrines, but they have also taught some strange things that many Mormon members are not aware of. Here are just a few:

- God the Father is not eternal and he has many wives.

- Jesus was conceived by way of a sexual relationship between God and Mary.

- Jesus was the spirit brother of Lucifer.

- Jesus Christ practiced polygamy during his ministry on earth.

- We are saved by grace, "after we have done all we can."

- Man is to be equal with God.

- All Christian denominations are not just wrong, but are an abomination to God.

The Book of Mormon is supposedly the lost story of America in which Joseph Smith claimed that a group of Israelites traveled to the Americas. Two major factions developed, and a great battle took place in Cumorah, New York, with over 200,000 men killed. After other conflicts, only one group survived, the Lamanites; and in the introduction of the Mormon Bible, it's claimed they were "the principal ancestors of the American Indians" (1981 edition).

In Texas, we have these huge gas stations called Buc-ees. A couple months ago, I was getting a coffee when I saw four young men with white shirts and ties. I immediately knew they were Mormons on their missionary trip. In east Texas, where boots and jeans are common, these guys certainly looked out of place! I knew they were members of the Church of Latter-Day Saints, so I said a quick prayer as I boldly initiated conversation.

"Hey guys! Nothing like Buc-ees! Y'all on a mission trip?"

"Yes, we are."

"Well, who has been on mission the longest?" I asked. I was friendly, but I was about to take control of the conversation. First, I got everyone's names. "I'm Dave. Matt, what do you want to study when you go to college?"

Matt responded, "Probably something in science."

"Interesting; there are so many possibilities in science. I have a question. If you believe that science is a noble field to go into, but from a scientific perspective, we don't have any DNA evidence that the American Indians came from the Israelites like your Book of Mormon teaches, how do you reconcile that? Also, your religion claims that there was a great battle in New York, but why hasn't compelling evidence been discovered?"

"I'm not sure; I think there may be some evidence, but I guess I just have faith!"

Immediately, another guy named Daniel interrupted, "If you go to this website, you'll find a lot of answers to your questions."

"Thank you for the card, Daniel. But look, I work in oncology diagnostics, and we must be very precise in diagnosing and treating particular cancerous biomarkers in patients. If we get it wrong, it can cost the patient's life. What about you? If something in science taught you something with certainty beyond a reasonable doubt that clearly and obviously contradicted what Joseph Smith told you in the Book of Mormon, would you look at your belief through the facts of science, or would you still hold onto the Book of Mormon?"

"No, I wouldn't believe the science, because I've prayed about it and have faith!"

I turned to Matt. "What about you?"

"Good question. I have to think about it. I might believe science."

"What about you other guys?" I asked.

Soon I had all four guys talking and even disagreeing with one another. I then calmly said, "Look, here's the difference between the Mormon concept of faith and my historic Christian faith. Mormons believe in blind faith, based on feelings, and burning in your bosoms if you prayed about something. But when I read the Bible, I'm not called to have blind faith, but to have faith only in that which I know to be true. Hebrews 11:6 says, 'Anyone who comes to God in faith must believe that he exists and he rewards those who earnestly seek him.' So first, we have an awareness of the reality, and then we step out in faith to commit to it. The foundation of my faith is not faith, but a historic event. That's why 1 Corinthians says, 'If Christ has not been raised from the dead, your faith is useless.' So if Christ really didn't rise again from the dead, then I wouldn't just be believing it in faith. Let's suppose you rigorously studied Mormonism from a historical standpoint and discovered many of the claims were false. Would you be willing to give up your faith in Mormonism?"

They disagreed with one another again and I smiled. "Guys, I want you to know that the Jesus I worship is real. Historically, there is overwhelming evidence that he rose again from the dead and proved his claim to be God, the I Am who revealed himself to Moses. I want to challenge you to go on a journey of examining the evidence of what's real and what's not real. Are you willing to do that?" One guy responded with a polite yes, while another challenged me to go to the Mormon website. We graciously said goodbye to each other, as I said a prayer in my heart for God to reveal himself to them.

Here are some good questions to ask Mormons:

- How do you define truth?
- You claim that American Indians came from Israelites, but what's the DNA evidence?
- If you weren't a Mormon, would you still believe in God? Why or why not?
- You claim that great civilizations lived in the Americas, but where is any archeological evidence? If there was a great battle in New York, why is there no evidence? What about all the cities mentioned in the Book of Mormon? Why haven't we discovered them, but we can go to Jerusalem and discover historical truths about Jesus?
- If Joseph Smith translated the Book of Mormon accurately by God's inspiration, then why were later revisions necessary?
- If you weren't a Mormon, would you still believe that Jesus is God and rose again from the dead? Why or why not?

Pantheism "Spirituality"

The word *pantheism* literally means "all [*pan*] is God [*theism*]."[7] Pantheism is a widespread spiritual belief. Two billion people on planet Earth—approximately one out of every three people in the word—is a pantheist. The two largest pantheistic religions are Hinduism and Buddhism. You will encounter many Hindus and Buddhists in America, and you'll meet Americans who have a smorgasbord of beliefs adapted from Hinduism, Christianity, and whatever pop culture pantheistic belief they've embraced. So, it's crucial for us to understand the dangers of this worldview and to realize why we need to trust the real Jesus.

Although there are differences among pantheistic views, most pantheists believe that God and the Universe are one and the same. Pantheism teaches that you must overcome the illusions of sense experience and trust the truth within yourself.

Many pantheists may not be aware of the history of their beliefs; in fact, they may be unfamiliar with the term "pantheism." Ted Cabal, a professor of philosophy at Southern Seminary, commented about some American pantheists:

> They prefer the practice of spirituality over organized religion. They believe that no single religious teacher can claim the allegiance of all; claims by Jesus as being *the* Way must be reinterpreted or rejected altogether. Mixing and matching the objects of worship, [pantheists] often identify themselves simultaneously in terms such as Buddhist, Jewish, and Presbyterian.[8]

Pantheism teaches that "everything is One," and "the One is God." It teaches that "I am God. You are God. The universe is God. We are all God."

The largest religion with a pantheistic worldview is Hinduism with 900,000,000 adherents, many living in India. From Zen Buddhism to the philosophy of G. W. F. Hegel, from many yoga classes at health clubs to the ideas of Oprah Winfrey, from movies like *Star Wars* to new age music and thousands of spiritual "self-help" and "inspirational" books, the pantheistic movement has always had its advocates. But the worldview has recently been spreading rapidly in the United States. In fact, many Christian leaders are beginning to incorporate pantheistic thought into their teaching without even recognizing it. We hear echoes of pantheistic thought in Christian churches when the lyrics of worship songs say things like, "God is the ground," "God is the air I breathe," and "God is the universe." When I was in seminary, Dr. Geisler expressed his concern about pantheistic ideas creeping into Christian churches. He encouraged worship leaders to be careful that their songs have words of truth. He said, "If you don't know the difference between 'God made the air' and 'God is the air,' you shouldn't be leading worship in church!" (I sure miss Dr. Geisler—who is in heaven now!) Pantheism is dangerous because it redefines most terms that Christians use.

Marianne Williamson has written a commentary on Helen Schucman's work *A Course in Miracles*. On *Oprah and Friends* XM radio, Williamson expressed her views, "My salvation comes from me. Nothing outside of me can hold me back. Within me is the world's salvation and my own." These teachings differ greatly from that of the New Testament, which says that salvation comes not from ourselves but from God, who is different from us.

Some good questions to ask a pantheist might include:

- How do you define truth?

- Are you spiritual or religious? What do you mean by spiritual?

- If Christianity was true, would you be willing to become a Christian?

- If everything is God, does that make Hitler God?

- If words are meaningless, then why do you read spiritual books?

- Historically, have you considered the evidence for the resurrection of Jesus?

In conclusion, true Christianity always stands out unique among other religions. There simply is no comparison!

Thus says the LORD, the King of Israel and his Redeemer, the LORD of hosts: "I am the first and I am the last; besides me there is no god. Who is like me? Let him proclaim it. . . . Is there a God besides me? There is no Rock; I know not any." (Isa. 44:6–8 ESV)

"Jesus Christ of Nazareth . . . there is salvation in no one else, for there is no other name under heaven given among men by which we must be saved." (Acts 4:10, 12 ESV)

You may easily forget details of other religions when you are engaged in conversations with these followers. If you can't remember specific questions, you can always use these three general questions with just about anybody who claims to be religious:

1. What do you think about Jesus Christ? He is the only religious leader who claimed he would rise again from the dead and then he did it! Do you think he actually did it? He also claimed to be God. Was he a deceiver? Just a madman who thought he was really God but wasn't?

2. In your religion, how do you know what will happen after you die? Do you have any assurance of being saved, of being right with God? If so, how?

3. Would you be willing to meet and study the Bible together?

11

YOU ARE GOD'S AMBASSADOR

The Bible uses various metaphors to describe those who follow Christ: we are like *soldiers* engaging in warfare; we are like *farmers* sowing seed and looking for a harvest; we are also called the *servants* of our Master, Jesus Christ, who want to please him as we serve him. I want us to look at one other metaphor that describes us as we seek to make an impact in the world around us—and that's the word *ambassador*.

Do you ever think of yourself as being an "ambassador for Jesus Christ"? Everywhere we go—whether it's because of work, or going out and having fun, participating in a sport, or attending a conference—we should think of ourselves as ambassadors of Jesus. This is what Paul wrote:

> Therefore, if anyone is in Christ, he is a new creation; the old has gone, the new has come! All this is from God, who reconciled us to himself through Christ and gave us the ministry of reconciliation: that God was reconciling the world to himself in Christ, not counting men's sins against them. And he has committed to us the message of reconciliation. We are therefore Christ's ambassadors, as though God were making his appeal through us. We implore you on Christ's behalf: Be reconciled to God. (2 Cor. 5:17–20)

What exactly is an ambassador? An ambassador is a duly authorized and appointed representative of one government sent to the government of a foreign country. Kings throughout history have used ambassadors: special messengers or envoys sent to bring important messages or negotiate a treaty. The United States has ambassadors to most countries with which we want or need to have diplomatic relations, but sometimes it takes a lot of courage to be an ambassador to a place where you may not be accepted.

John Adams, before becoming the second president of the United States, had challenges as ambassador while serving President George Washington and the newly formed nation. His time in France was difficult, because he spoke very little French and seemed unintelligent to some of the elite politicians at Versailles who wanted to hear from the more fluent Benjamin Franklin. Later, Adams was commissioned by President Washington to meet with King George III, the very king whom the Americans had declared and fought war against. One author wrote,

> Both men pulled off what could have been a very awkward interview with considerable grace. The king was frank in telling Adams he had not consented to American independence but he now accepted it, and he ended by inviting Adams to visit his extensive library.[1]

As ambassadors of Jesus Christ, God has commissioned you and me for a duty even greater than that of John Adams meeting with King George III. Jesus gave his followers a commission that applies to us today:

> Then Jesus came to them and said, "All authority in heaven and on earth has been given to me. Therefore go and make disciples of all nations." (Matt. 28:18–19)

So, as we go, we have no authority of our own. We have only delegated authority; we stand only in the place of Jesus. This is what it means to speak "in Jesus' name." If God ever uses us to heal a sick person or do a great work in his name, it's not by any power of our own; it's only by the authority of Jesus.

> "I have given you authority to trample on snakes and scorpions and to overcome all the power of the enemy; nothing will harm you." (Luke 10:19)

Every Christ follower, therefore, ought to live in this world as God's duly appointed representative. Ambassadors spend much time in countries that are not their home country. When I have traveled to Africa, Russia, or Canada, people frequently assume because of my accent or mannerism that I'm an American. But I'm not going there just to represent the United States. I am there to proclaim the gospel and to train pastors and young leaders in biblical discipleship and apologetics.

In my full-time day job in medical sales, I constantly encounter nurses, doctors, and coworkers who may hold to a different religion or be outspoken about their atheism or new age meditation. Whenever I've given lectures at universities such as Duke, University of Virginia, or Yale University on ethical issues like abortion, natural law, or what it means to be human, I realize that my beliefs aren't going to be popular with every single student or faculty member.

Likewise, in various walks of your life, being a Christian may not be very popular. You may be pressured by your company to participate in events with which you don't agree. Your beliefs and my beliefs will be hated by many in the world. We're living in a time in which people will say, "It's fine for you to tell me your story and your beliefs about Jesus, so long as you don't impose your beliefs on me or others."

We live in a society where you may suffer persecution for standing up for what you believe to be right. Even though Christianity is spreading more rapidly worldwide than ever before, there are still many who will repudiate those of us who claim that Jesus Christ is exclusively the way to God.

In today's atmosphere of growing intolerance toward exclusivity, followers of Christ must have a strong foundation of knowing the historical Jesus (who, by the way, was Eastern not Western). If we're ridiculed or even hated for our faith, we must have a base of knowledge that's unshakable. Let us therefore keep in mind these words from Jesus:

"Do not be surprised, my brothers, if the world hates you."

(1 John 3:13)

"We are aliens and strangers in the world." (1 Pet. 2:11)

"We are temporary residents and foreigners." (1 Pet. 2:11 NLT)

These words imply that this world is not where our roots are to be; I like best the expression "temporary residents." One day, you may have to decide that you need to leave your job in order to follow Jesus. If you're not very happy here in this world, are you longing for something better? We're like people passing through who haven't yet found the place that will be our final home. We can never be completely at home in this present culture. There's a lot of sadness as I write this because of the coronavirus, school cancellations, drops in the stock market, and various other uncertainties. Yes, we want to work hard and be optimistic to pull through, find cures, and help the needy, but we know that this life is not all there is.

They admitted that they were aliens and strangers on earth. . . . They were longing for a better country—a heavenly one.

(Heb. 11:13–16)

This is one reason we Christians should never lose our joy over political or economic events or negative news. We need to reevaluate our own lives. Are we really "longing for a better country"? As Paul says, "Our citizenship [homeland] is in heaven" (Phil. 3:20). We are Christ's ambassadors, so let's act like it!

Ambassadors Are Sent to Do What the Sovereign Leader Would Do If Present

Scripture says, "As He is, so also are we in this world" (1 John 4:17 NAS). Although I'm now in medical sales and no longer working in what some would call "full-time ministry," I'm still in ministry through my work. I'm not just a representative of a biotech company; I'm an ambassador of Jesus.

As I travel and meet with people, I ask myself, "What would Christ do?" What would an ambassador such as Billy Graham do in this situation? Do we act as Jesus would act? Do we serve as Jesus would serve? One translation puts it this way: "We are Christ's personal representatives" (2 Cor. 5:20 Phillips). This ought to be a most sobering thought: *We are Christ's personal representatives.* The world doesn't need more preachers, but it does need Christ's representatives in every walk of life—medicine, sports, business, or elsewhere. We can change this world for Christ in every area of our lives.

Ambassadors Ought to Be Good Examples of What They Represent

Paul said, "Follow my example, as I follow the example of Christ" (1 Cor. 11:1). There's a bumper sticker I don't like that says, *Christians aren't perfect; they're just forgiven.* To me, it sounds as if it's okay when we sin. Many of our contemporary Christian worship songs seem to be about how broken and messed up we are. Is this how we view the Christian life? Some may interpret this as we're forgiven, so it really doesn't matter how we live our lives. No, none of us are perfect, but we ought to at least seek to be an *example* of our Savior (1 Cor. 11:1; 1 Pet. 2:21).

People need real-life demonstrations of imperfect people who are serious and committed to their faith. We need to be victorious and confident in Christ and not wallow in our struggles. Some may say we need to be "authentic," but there's nothing "authentic" about continuing in our sin.

Ambassadors Are More Diplomatic than Confrontational in Their Approach

Proverbs 15:18 says, "You can catch more flies with honey than vinegar." When U.S. ambassadors visit another country, they may at times confront a matter or issue a warning. But most of the time, they are engaged in relaxed conversation, not hard confrontation. In his book *Tactics*, Greg Koukl says he believes we should generally try to be diplomatic. He calls this the "Ambassador Model."[2] Paul sometimes confronted religious people, but he was not generally harsh; he was gentle in his conversations. Note these examples:

> As apostles of Christ we could have been a burden to you, but we were gentle among you, like a mother caring for her little children. (1 Thess. 2:6–7)

> And the Lord's servant must not quarrel; instead, he must be kind to everyone, able to teach, not resentful. Those who oppose him he must gently instruct, in the hope that God will grant them repentance leading them to a knowledge of the truth, and that they will come to their senses. (2 Tim. 2:24–26)

Ambassadors Are Not Sent to Promote Their Own Welfare or Honor

We are to seek the honor of God alone, not our own honor.

> Am I now trying to win the approval of men, or of God? Or am I trying to please men? If I were still trying to please men, I would not be a servant of Christ. (Gal.1:10)

Even the best ambassadors at times will be disliked and rejected. Do you worry too much about people liking you? Are we overly concerned with how people respond to our social media posts? Do we get mad at the whole church or workplace because a few people gossiped negatively about us? If you're too concerned about this, you won't be an effective ambassador of Jesus. We should never let approval of others be our focus; we need to seek to please God.

I'm impressed with the bravery of spiritual ambassadors despite great personal dangers. As Christ's ambassadors, we're not survivalists seeking to save ourselves from all harm. This means that people are ready to listen to the good news we offer. We seek to live for Christ and promote Christ. If we pay a price for that, then so be it. "If God is for us, who can be against us?" (Rom.8:31).

Lastly, Ambassadors Are Knowledgeable and Clear Concerning the Message They Bring

We don't need to be great theologians or philosophers or have great knowledge, but we ought to have some knowledge and should challenge ourselves to grow intellectually. Do you study the Bible? Have you considered taking an evening course in apologetics or attending an apologetics conference? Ambassadors aren't wishy-washy, cowardly, or compromising. They're enthusiastic and confident about what or who they represent.

By the grace of God, we Christians have been introduced to the most wonderful and the greatest king in the universe: King Jesus! We don't need to be ashamed; we don't need to be afraid to compare him to any other king. We ought to be proud to represent him. As ambassadors, we can be courteous and tactful, yet also be bold and enthusiastic about what we believe.

Paul said, "I am an ambassador in chains. Pray that I may declare [the gospel] fearlessly, as I should" (Eph. 6:20). Being in a cold, rat-infested Roman prison cell would be one of the last places anyone would want to end up. Notice Paul's attitude, though. He doesn't pray for release or a pardon from Caesar; he doesn't pray for personal peace and joy. Why? He realized that even in undesirable situations, *he was Christ's ambassador*. He prayed for only one thing: that he might have boldness to declare the good news of Christ.

How do you see your circumstances? Don't like them? Do you fuss and complain? Do you think you need to change something or move somewhere to be an ambassador of Christ? Paul says no!

> Nevertheless, each one should retain the place in life that the Lord assigned to him and to which God has called him.
>
> (1 Cor. 7:17)

When Paul was in that prison, he revealed how he saw his circumstances:

> I have learned the secret of being content in any and every situation, whether well fed or hungry, whether living in plenty or in want. I can do everything through him who gives me strength. (Phil. 4:12–13)

Contentment doesn't mean we never seek to improve our situation; it means that when our situation doesn't improve, we can still maintain a peace and satisfaction in the Lord; we can pray, "Lord, if this is where you've destined me to be, then I won't give way to a complaint of self-pity; I will be content and give thanks, even in this circumstance."

Ambassadors of Jesus Bring the Message of Reconciliation

"To reconcile" means to restore friendship, to make a former enemy into a friend. This is exactly what God has done with us through Jesus.

> Since we have now been justified by his blood, how much more shall we be saved from God's wrath through him! For if, when we were God's enemies, we were reconciled to him through the death of his Son, how much more, having been reconciled, shall we be saved through his life! (Rom. 5:9–10)

Our friendship with God was restored by the death of his Son while we were still his enemies. (Rom. 5:10 NLT)

As you go to work every day, may you have a renewed sense of being an ambassador for the kingdom of God! Whether it's going to school or relating to a neighbor or a relative, you represent King Jesus and the greatest government ever—the kingdom of God! Even with your flaws and shortcomings, will you allow God to use you to point others to Christ?

A documentary on the life of Billy Graham is aptly titled *God's Ambassador*.[3] Here's a quote from Mr. Graham's autobiography that I think reveals a great attitude and one we should seek to emulate:

I never go to see important people—or anyone else—without having the deep realization that I am—first and foremost—an ambassador of the King of kings and Lord of lords. From the moment I enter the room, I am thinking about how I can get the conversation around to the Gospel. We may discuss a dozen other things first, but I am always thinking of ways I can share Christ and His message of hope with them.[4]

As we go out to engage in conversations about Jesus, may we all have a sense of our calling on our lives. We are no ordinary workers, no ordinary students, no ordinary parents, no ordinary singles—we are his ambassadors! We pray, we go, and we grow as we go.

God, we pray that you will help us to be faithful to your call on our lives, and to be more alert to share this wonderful news of Jesus! Amen!

Notes

Chapter 1

1. See https://www.barna.com/research/half-churchgoers-not -heard-great-commission.

2. "The State of the Church in 2016," Barna Group, https://www.barna .com/research/state-church-2016.

Chapter 2

1. Nancy Gibbs and Richard Ostling, "God's Bully Pulpit," *Time* (November 15, 1993).

2. Mark Cahill, *One Thing You Can't Do in Heaven*, 5th ed. (Rockwell, TX: Biblical Discipleship, 2011), 33.

3. George Barna, "Almost Half of Practicing Christian Millennials Say Evangelism Is Wrong," https://www.barna.com/research /millennials-oppose-evangelism/.

4. Penn Jillette, "A Gift of a Bible," https://www.youtube.com /watch?v=6md638smQd8.

5. Ruth Alexander, "Are There Really 100,000 New Christian Martyrs Every Year?" BBC News, November 12, 2013, https://www.bbc.com/news /magazine-24864587.

6. Dwight Lyman Moody, *One Thousand and One Thoughts from My Library* (New York: Fleming H. Revell Company, 1898).

Chapter 3

1. Gloria Furman, "How to Start a Conversation about Jesus," *Desiring God* (blog), November 7, 2018, https://www.desiringgod.org/articles /how-to-start-a-conversation-about-jesus.

2. *The Gospel of John*, directed by David Batty (Netflix, 2014), DVD.

3. Mary Beth Marklein, "More Students Coming (and Going) Overseas for College," *USA Today*, November 11, 2013, www.usatoday.com/story /news/nation/2013/11/11/international-students-and-study-abroad/3442733.

4. Kevin G. Harney, *Organic Outreach for Ordinary People: Sharing Good News Naturally* (Grand Rapids: Zondervan, 2009), 21.

5. *Unplanned: What She Saw Changed Everything*, directed by Cary Solomon and Chuck Konzelman (Scottsdale, AZ: Pure Flix, 2019), DVD.

Chapter 4

1. Alison Wood Brooks and Leslie K. John, "The Surprising Power of Questions," *Harvard Business Review* (May/June 2018), https://hbr .org/2018/05/the-surprising-power-of-questions.html.

2. Brooks and John, "The Surprising Power of Questions."

3. Brooks and John, "The Surprising Power of Questions."

4. Brooks and John, "The Surprising Power of Questions."

5. Greg Koukl, *Tactics: A Game Plan for Discussing Your Christian Convictions* (Grand Rapids: Zondervan, 2019), 55.

6. Dave Sterrett, ed., *We Choose Life: Authentic Stories, Movements of Hope* (Peabody, MA: Hendrickson, 2016).

7. Leslie K. John and Alison Wood Brooks, "Ask Better Questions," *Harvard Business Review*, HBR IdeaCast / Episode 631 (podcast), https:// hbr.org/ideacast/2018/05/ask-better-questions.html.

Chapter 5

1. "The Bridge to Life," The Navigators, https://www.navigators.org /resource/the-bridge-to-life. From *The Bridge to Life* (Colorado Springs: NavPress, 2020). See also "One-Verse Evangelism: How to Share Christ's Love Conversationally & Visually," The Navigators, https://www.naviga-tors.org/resource/one-verse-evangelism. From *One-Verse Evangelism* by Randy D. Raysbrook (Colorado Springs: NavPress, 2000).

2. Dave Sterrett, *The Bridge Gospel Illustration*, Disruptive Truth (video), https://www.youtube.com/watch?v=7groxXfR3L8.

3. Thomas Nagel, *The Last Word* (Oxford: Oxford University Press, 1997), 127.

4. D. James Kennedy, *Evangelism Explosion: Equipping Churches for Friendship, Evangelism, Discipleship, and Healthy Growth* (Carol Stream, IL: Tyndale House, 1996), 75.

Chapter 7

1. R. C. Sproul, *Now That's a Good Question!* (Wheaton, IL: Tyndale Publishers, 1996), 14.

2. See Mark 14:62; Titus 2:13; Rom. 9:5; Heb. 1:8; Phil. 2:6 ("equal" is the same Greek word as in John 5:18); Col. 2:9.

3. Gary R. Habermas and Michael R. Licona, *The Case for the Resurrection* (Grand Rapids: Kregel, 2004), 49.

4. See Francis J. Beckwith, William Lane Craig, and J. P. Moreland, eds. *To Everyone an Answer: A Case for the Christian Worldview* (Downers Grove, IL: InterVarsity Press, 2009), 182.

5. For examples, see Gerd Lüdemann, *The Resurrection of Jesus: A Historical Inquiry* (Buffalo, NY: Prometheus, 2004); and Michael Goulder, "The Baseless Fabric of a Vision," in Gavin D'Costa, ed., *Resurrection Reconsidered* (Oxford: Oneworld, 1996), 48–61. Both agree that this resurrection idea was a tradition taught *within a few years* of Jesus' death.

6. Flavius Josephus, *The Works of Flavius Josephus*, trans. William Whiston (Auburn, NY: John E. Bardsley, 1895), 119. See also *The Works of Josephus*, ed. and trans. William Whiston (Peabody, MA: Hendrickson, 1987).

7. Peter Kreeft, "Why I Believe Jesus Is the Son of God," in *Why I Am a Christian: Leading Thinkers Explain Why They Believe*, ed. Norman L. Geisler and Paul K. Hoffman (Grand Rapids: Baker Books, 2001), 250.

8. Marty Angelo, "How Chuck Colson's Legacy of Hope Lives On," *Prison Fellowship* (blog), https://www.prisonfellowship.org/2018/04/chuck-colsons-legacy-hope-lives/.

Chapter 8

1. Walter Isaacson, *Steve Jobs* (New York: Simon & Schuster, 2011).

Chapter 9

1. Friedrich Nietzsche, *Thus Spoke Zarathustra: A Book for All and None* (1885) cited in *The Portable Nietzsche*, ed. and trans. Walter Kaufmann (NY: Penguin Books, 1982), https://antilogicalism.files.wordpress.com/2017/07/the-portable-nietzsche-walter-kaufmann.pdf.

2. Richard Dawkins, *River Out of Eden: A Darwinian Perspective* (New York: Harper Collins, 1996), 133.

3. William Lane Craig, *On Guard* (Colorado Springs: David C. Cook, 2010), 132.

4. C. S. Lewis, *Mere Christianity* (New York: HarperOne, 1952), 6.

5. Martin Luther King, Jr., "Rediscovering Lost Values," The Martin Luther King, Jr. Research and Education Institute, Stanford University (speech given at Second Baptist Church, Detroit, February 28, 1954), https://kinginstitute.stanford.edu/king-papers/documents/rediscovering-lost-values-0. Published in *The Papers of Martin Luther King, Jr. Volume II: Rediscovering Precious Values, July 1951–November 1955*, ed. Clayborne Carson, Ralph Luker, Penny A. Russell, and Peter Holloran (Berkeley: University of California Press, 1994).

6. John Hill Burton, *Life and Correspondence of David Hume: From the Papers Bequeathed by His Nephew to the Royal Society of Edinburgh; and Other Original Sources* (London: W. Tait, 1846), 97.

7. Roger Penrose and Stephen Hawking, *The Nature of Space and Time* (Princeton: Princeton University Press, 2010), 20.

8. Robert Jastrow, "Have Astronomers Found God?," *Time* (June 25, 1978), https://www.nytimes.com/1978/06/25/archives/have-astronomers-found-god-theologians-are-delighted-that-the.html.

9. William Paley, *Natural Theology: Or Evidences of the Existence and Attributes of the Deity* (London: W. S. Orr & Company, 1837), 6.

10. "From DNA to Protein," Your Genome (video), https://www.youtube.com/watch?v=gG7uCskUOrA.

11. Francis Collins, *The Language of God: A Scientist Presents Evidence for Belief* (New York: Simon & Schuster, 2008), 2.

12. Antony Flew and Gary Habermas, "My Pilgrimage from Atheism to Theism: A Discussion between Antony Flew and Gary Habermas," *Evangelical Philosophical Society* (EPS Article Library, 2004), https://www.epsociety.org/library/articles.asp?pid=33.

Chapter 10

1. Nabeel Qureshi, *Seeking Allah, Finding Jesus: A Devout Muslim Encounters Christianity* (Grand Rapids: Zondervan, 2018).

2. Norman L. Geisler, *Systematic Theology: In One Volume* (Grand Rapids: Baker, 2011).

3. Lee Strobel, *The Case for Faith: A Journalist Investigates the Toughest Objections to Christianity* (Grand Rapids: Zondervan, 2014), 162.

4. Visit their website at www.israelcollective.org.

5. Qureshi, *Seeking Allah, Finding Jesus*, 225.

6. Qur'an, *sūrah* 4 (*an-Nisā*) *āyāt* 157–158.

7. Norman L. Geisler, *Baker Encyclopedia of Christian Apologetics* (Grand Rapids: Baker, 1998), 580.

8. Ted Cabal, "How Should a Christian Relate to the New Age Movement?," *The Apologetics Study Bible* (Nashville: B&H, 2017), 1784.

Chapter 11

1. "9 Notable Ambassadors in History," *HistoryExtra*, July 30, 2019, https://www.historyextra.com/period/second-world-war/ambassador-history-chapuys-macartney-adams/.

2. Koukl, *Tactics*, 20.

3. *Billy Graham: God's Ambassador*, directed by Michael Merriman (Gaither Film Productions, 2006), DVD.

4. Billy Graham, *Just As I Am: The Autobiography of Billy Graham* (New York: HarperOne, 1997), 684.